Testimonials

'When I first started reading Banish the Bitch, I was sceptical to say the least. I thought it was going to be another one of those boring dating books. I'm happy to say it's not! It's way more than that. I'm blown away.'

– Christina Rice

'Where has this information been all my life? I wish I had read this book 20 years ago. As soon as I started reading, I was hooked.'

– Jenny Heydon

'Banish The Bitch is about men but it's also about how to balance your own masculine and feminine energy. At different periods in my life, I felt I needed to be with a man. That was my own bullshit and I see that clearly now. After reading Banish The Bitch, I feel empowered and at peace with who I am.'

– Nicole Barrett

"Sex in the City meets personal development"

Find Your **Mr Right**

BANISH the BITCH and BRING out the BABE

The **New Rules** for Finding Love

Lisa B.

Disclaimer

All the information and concepts contained within this publication are of the nature of general comment only and are not in any way recommended as individual advice. The intent is to offer a variety of information to provide a wider range of choices now and in the future, recognising that we all have widely diverse circumstances and viewpoints.

Should any reader choose to make use of the information contained herein, this is their decision, and the contributors (and their companies), authors and publishers do not assume any responsibilities whatsoever under any condition or circumstances. It is recommended that the reader obtain their own independent advice.

All names that appear in this publication have been changed for privacy reasons and each story is the author's interpretation of the facts.

First Edition 2016

Copyright © 2016 by Lisa B

All rights reserved. No part of this publication may be reproduced, stored in a retrieval system, or transmitted in any form or by any means, electronic, mechanical, photocopying, recording or otherwise, without the prior written permission from the author.

National Library of Australia Cataloguing-in-Publication entry

Creator: B., Lisa, author.

Title: Banish the bitch and bring out the babe : the new rules for

finding love / Lisa B.

ISBN: 9781925471052 (paperback)

Subjects: Women--Identity.
Women--Sexual behavior.
Femininity.
Love.
Man-woman relationships.

Dewey Number: 305.4

Published with support by Author Express
www.authorexpress.com

For all enquiries please contact Lisa B. support@lisab.com.au

Dedication

I would like to dedicate this book to Anthony Robbins.

My journey into self-help and self-awareness started many many years ago when I bought Tony Robbins tapes through a television infomercial. I then went to years of Tony's seminars. I participated, I crewed, I did leadership and Platinum Partners. I did everything to absorb Tony's content.

From having Tony's teachings in my life, I have always felt a level of confidence and certainty. I know that no matter how bad things get, I have the resources inside of me to deal with whatever life throws at me.

I have done so many things in my life that I would never have thought were possible all because of the mindset I adopted.

To the things I learnt. To the risks I have taken. To the many friends I have made through your seminars. To the fantastic life I have had.

Thank you Tony.

Acknowledgements

I want to start by thanking my parents for being amazing role models – happily married for over fifty years. My parents, unfortunately, never got to see this book in real life, but I know they're watching over Max and I always.

I also wish to acknowledge those who were there for me during some of life's bumpy rides. The first is my son, Max, the most amazing and incredible, little boy in the whole world. Max, I am so proud of you every single day. I love you with all of my heart and soul – always remember the sea turtles.

Next is My Mr Big – words cannot express how eternally grateful I am for having you in my life. Thank you for everything. I love you.

Thank you to Fiona Jones from Authors Express. You are simply amazing! You have changed my world!

My brother Rodney Whyte, my brother-in-law David Volke, my friends Laurie Driggers, Lulu Wren, Maryanne Kourouche, Kim Johnson, Daryl Apps, Naomi Rogers Twyford, Julia Melinek and Kat Heart – thanks for being there, and thanks for listening. I love you all.

Contents

Introduction 1
   Rediscovering your feminine energy 3
   If only I knew then what I know now... 6
   How I grew massive testicles 8
   It's time to meet your white knight 11

Before we start 13

All about you

Chapter 1: Feminine energy 19
   What is feminine energy? 20
   How will adopting feminine energy enhance your life? 24
   Why do we resist feminine energy? 25
   How do you step into your feminine energy? 31

Chapter 2: Masculine energy 47
   What is masculine energy? 47
   Why is masculine energy important? 51
   Why do we resist our masculine energy? 52
   How do you transform into masculine energy? ... 54

Chapter 3: Integration — 63
- The need for integration — 65
- How to integrate both energies — 70

Finding Mr Right

Chapter 4: Polarity and attraction — 87
- Why is polarity important? — 90
- Creating polarity — 91
- Maintaining polarity — 101

Chapter 5: Prepare for the man of your dreams — 111
- One minute you are happy… — 112
- Tackle your relationship patterns — 113
- Adopt an abundance mentality — 119
- Get clear on what you want — 120
- Who do you need to become? — 125
- Protect yourself — 128

Chapter 6: Enter the dating game — 133
- Fish where the fish are — 134
- Building attraction — 135
- Is he relationship material? — 138
- Becoming 'exclusive' — 144
- Dealing with rejection — 148
- Dating and relationship tips — 149

You and Him

Chapter 7: Your relationship foundations – How to keep your soul mate — **157**
- The foundations of your relationship — 158
- Communication — 160
- Love — 166
- Intimacy — 172
- Values — 177
- Common goals — 183

Chapter 8: If things go wrong — **187**
- Interdependent relationships — 188
- Affairs – just don't do it! — 190

Chapter 9: Relationship breakdowns — **201**
- The 4Rs of deterioration — 202
- The options — 204

Chapter 10: Self-love, self-esteem and self-confidence — **219**
- The four love buckets and how to fill them — 220
- Reclaim your identity — 231
- Build your self-esteem and self-confidence — 236

Conclusion: It's your time — **253**

A message for you... — **257**

About the author — **259**

Bonus
A special gift for you

We would love you to continue The Banish The Bitch online experience

Please go to

www.BanishTheBitch.com/freechapteronline

To claim your free gifts.

Introduction

Surrender to what is. Let go of what was.
Have faith in what will be.

– Sonia Ricotti

For the first ten years of my quest to learn about masculine and feminine energy, I thought that I had to banish my masculine energy. I thought I had to become feminine.

I was so wrong.

What I discovered was much more powerful than I could ever have imagined.

Are you looking for love?

I've found there are five types of women searching for love:

1. She would love to be in a relationship, but she won't settle for just anyone. She's hoping to find the perfect man for her.
2. She's so desperate to be with someone that she'll try hard to hang onto *anyone*, even if she knows he's not the right one for her.
3. She really wants a man but doesn't know what to do. She puts on a brave front. She's smart, she has a great personality, she's independent and she's *alone*. She may tell everyone that she

Banish The Bitch And Bring Out The Babe

likes it that way. She may also tell everyone that she doesn't have time for a relationship because she's too set in her ways and she likes her freedom. Besides, there are no good men out there anyway. The truth is, saying that is just easier than putting herself out there. Secretly, she may be sad and feeling lonely, but she doesn't know where to start.

4. She would love to be with someone but she's still hurting from past relationships. Whether she was betrayed or she's lost the love of her life, she's scared to commit again.

5. She's in a relationship that has lost its passion and now she's wondering if she can rekindle the spark. She may feel like she is drowning in a loveless relationship. They may have loved each other dearly at one point only to one day wake up and discover they have grown apart. They may have realised that they are on two completely different paths.

Does this sound familiar?

Regardless of which woman you may relate to, there's one thing they all have in common – they want to find love and fulfilment through an intimate relationship. Yet, with today's divorce rate approaching fifty percent, only two of them are likely to find what they want and have it last.

Why is this statistic so high? The reason, I believe, is because so many of us choose the wrong partner in the first place. We get caught up with whom we are with and the fairy tale it could be. We envision a beautiful wedding, we feel grown up and we begin our new lives as adults. We don't really think about the future.

Most of us have higher expectations for our business or professional lives. Many of us prioritise recognition and monetary success over our personal lives, as money is a tangible reward that demonstrates how hard we've worked. On the flip side, we tend to have low expectations for our relationships or we take them for granted. As a result, we don't often spend the time to first choose the right partner, and to then nourish our relationships.

Introduction

Women's liberation went a long way to achieving equal rights for women, giving us access to more independence, strength and freedom of choice than ever before. We are told that we can be and do whatever we want. We can build our own empires and make our own choices. We don't *have* to be with a man, unlike earlier generations; we can instead *choose* to be with a man.

This book is about choice – your right to choose.

A woman can have a career, a voice and a brain. And over the past few decades, most of us have been conditioned to focus on that strong, determined and driven side of ourselves rather than the softer, more nurturing side that yearns to experience love and connection.

Ultimately, we feel more comfortable about wanting material things than we do about wanting a fantastic relationship with our partner. Yet, if we delved truly and deeply into our hearts for a moment, wouldn't we realise that's what everyone wants? To feel loved at the deepest level. The trouble is that we're so busy trying to impress people we don't like, to buy things we can't afford and to add more achievements to our CVs that we forget about our need for love and connection.

What happened?

We lost touch with our feminine energy.

Rediscovering your feminine energy

The focus on doing, achieving and getting can be very effective. You may have been promoted, landed big deals, negotiated contracts and more as a result. It's probably one of the reasons for your success to date.

However, what if I told you that this focus could be damaging your love life? What if I told you it could be turning off the very men you want to attract, or changing the dynamic in your current relationship?

Banish The Bitch And Bring Out The Babe

How does this work?

At a basic level, we have two types of energy in our relationships and in life. Throughout this book I'll be referring to them as masculine and feminine energy, but if you are uncomfortable with the terminology, 'masculine energy' can be replaced with the words 'strong energy' or 'power energy'. 'Feminine energy' can be replaced with the words 'soft energy' or 'loving energy'.

Masculine energy is focused, controlling and action-oriented. Masculine focuses on solving problems, getting results and building empires. Feminine energy, on the other hand, is free-flowing, joyful and loving. She is connected to herself, the moment, the people around her and nature. Where masculine energy focuses on *doing*, feminine energy is all about *being* and *feeling*.

Imagine that masculine energy is a car and feminine energy is the road. Masculine energy sets the direction – he knows where he wants to go and he aims to get them there. Feminine energy creates variety and excitement. She is the unpredictable terrain. She can offer a bumpy ride, she can be fast, she can be spontaneous, she can be calm and she can be wild.

How do these energies affect us in life?

- **In ourselves** – We need to have masculine and feminine energy in our own bodies in order to feel balance.

- **In our relationships** – We need to have masculine and feminine energy in our relationships to ensure we have balance and polarity with our partner.

In the working world, high-powered corporate women are rewarded greatly for using their masculine energy. They are rewarded for their power, their tough decision-making and the way they fight for what they believe in. They're rewarded massively for being strong.

What many women don't realise is that carrying this same masculine energy into the quest to find a loving relationship will make it virtually impossible for them to attract a masculine man.

Why? Because passionate relationships require both energies – masculine energy as well as feminine energy. This is why those who are masculine in their energy are attracted to those who are feminine in their energy, and vice versa.

We need to have both energies represented in a relationship to create polarity – this attraction or chemistry will help keep a relationship passionate. On the other hand, without this polarity, two people will lack any chemistry to begin with, or any spark will quickly fizzle out.

Ultimately, if you're in your masculine energy with men, you won't attract a masculine man. Your energy will be too similar to his, so instead of seeing you as girlfriend material, he'll relate to you more like one of his friends. There will be no sexual attraction or chemistry. Instead, you'll attract men in their feminine energy.

As a side note, if you identify that you have predominantly masculine energy, the question becomes whether that is your true energy, or whether it is a mask you have been wearing. If it is a mask, you can adjust back to your true self if that's what you want. However, if you do feel this is you, I'm not telling you to become someone you are not. I'll simply be inviting you to explore another part of yourself. It's really up to you to choose which energy you would like to wield.

In this book I'll refer to 'feminine energy' and 'the feminine' to represent the feminine energy in a relationship, and 'masculine energy' and 'the masculine' to represent the masculine energy in a relationship. 'The masculine' could be a woman or a man displaying masculine energy, and 'the feminine' could be a woman or a man displaying feminine energy.

At times, I will refer to the woman as the feminine element of a relationship and the man as the masculine element; however, keep in mind that the roles can just as easily be switched. The same goes for same-sex relationships, where two people of the same gender will each represent different energies. The key takeaway is that, in any passionate relationship, each person takes on one of these energetic roles.

Banish The Bitch And Bring Out The Babe

The role you choose initially will determine the partner you attract, and how you manage to maintain the polarity long-term could determine the longevity of your relationship.

Once you understand the differences between masculine and feminine energy, you'll have a more comprehensive understanding of yourself *and* the men in your life. You will be able to access whichever energy you need for any given situation, and you will have the ability to form deeper relationships and friendships with people in both energies.

> *In order to take care of ourselves and have balance in our lives, we must integrate our masculine and feminine energy.*

If only I knew then what I know now…

I remember going to a party when I was eighteen, and a woman asked me my age. When I told her, she laughed and said, 'If only I knew then what I know now.'

It *really* made me curious as to what I could learn from others, those who had been successful and those who had made mistakes.

With this in mind, *Banish the Bitch and Bring Out the Babe* will give you the information you need to avoid making some potentially huge mistakes. It will also help you to see where you may have gone wrong in past relationships, and it will help to guide you in the right direction. At the end of every chapter, I will share my quick tips, entitled: *If only I knew then what I know now…* inspired by the lady I met when I was eighteen.

How does *Banish the Bitch* work? This book is broken into three parts.

Part 1 – You. This is all about *you* – your feminine energy, your masculine energy and how to integrate the two to create a rich and fulfilling life complete with amazing relationships. Accessing your masculine energy will *empower* you to get things done and stand up for yourself, while accessing your feminine energy will allow you relax and experience love and connection. Integrating the two will set the stage for attracting your Mr Right.

Part 2 – Finding Mr Right. Here, I'll dive deep into polarity and how masculine and feminine energy interact in a relationship, teaching you how to create polarity to attract the man of your dreams. Then you'll learn how to become the woman who will attract the right men by addressing your relationship beliefs and getting clear on what you want, followed by some practical dating advice.

Part 3 – You and Him. I will focus on you as a couple and how to maintain the spark once you're already in a relationship. If you're in a relationship that has lost its sizzle, or you just want to make sure you sustain it once you meet Mr Right, here is where you'll learn about the foundations of any successful relationship, why it's so important to maintain your sense of self, your patterns and beliefs, what to do when things go wrong and how to tell if it's time to let go and move on.

This book is going to help you to focus on becoming deliriously happy, centred and balanced. I'm going to help you feel an unshakable confidence in *you*, so much so that you won't ever feel like you *need* to be with a man. Instead, you will want to be with a man, which will give you the power to *choose* the right one for you.

Together, we will explore your current situation and you will discover choices you may not have known you had. We will set the course for a relationship you love, rather than being stuck in a relationship because you feel you have to be.

If you're single, you'll gain the tools to find the perfect man for you. If you believe you're in the wrong relationship, you'll gain the confidence to move on. If you're in the right relationship but it's lost its spark, you'll learn new ways to ignite your passion.

How do I know this? I lived it.

How I grew massive testicles

Since 1994, I've studied human motivation and I've read hundreds of books on the subject. I studied psychology at university for two years. I'm an accredited life coach, an accredited Neuro-linguistic Programming (NLP) practitioner, and I've also operated my own training businesses.

In my past life, though, I worked in real estate, buying my own office at the age of twenty-three with big expectations. I *knew* I was going to be a huge success – I was committed to mastering my career, I worked hard and I was driven to succeed. Work was my life, and it stayed that way for the next decade. Up until I turned thirty-four, I worked like crazy. I worked seven days a week and I simply forgot how to live. When I wasn't at work, my mind was.

I still remember waking up on my thirty-fourth birthday thinking how quickly my life had 'happened'. I'd worked hard and I had material possessions, but I didn't have the love I craved.

I didn't realise at the time that my incredible focus made me very masculine in my energy, both at work and at home. While my masculine energy served me extremely well in my business life, it did not really serve me in my personal life.

Mr Beige

Mr Beige and I first started dating when I was only fourteen and he was sixteen. Back then, he played football, he rode motorbikes and he was totally masculine in his core. He was disciplined, smart and strong. When we worked together in our business, we were extremely successful because of our differences. He loved paperwork, graphs and taxation and I loved dealing with people. However, even though he was very masculine, I became the masculine force in the business.

The business was *my* dream, *my* vision and *my* passion. I found that it massively filled my needs – I received lots of recognition and fantastic financial rewards. I wanted to live to my potential and work is where all of my focus went. I wanted the freedom to do whatever I wanted, whenever I wanted. I also needed to have a purpose. I was like a freight train, determined to achieve my goals.

I started making a lot of the decisions myself, and then a lot more of the decisions, and then *all* of the decisions. If there was a problem, I had already figured out the solution and acted on it before he even knew there was a problem. Before long, the only role he felt comfortable in was the role of the 'pleaser'.

I can see now that Mr Beige really didn't know what to do. He probably felt like he had no choice but to jump on the train. My vision was so big it became *our* vision.

Meanwhile, in order to run the business, I felt that I had to compete with all the men in the business world, and I built barrier after barrier of protection. This transferred over into my personal life, where I saw men as competition. Sometimes I treated them like they were worthy opponents, but most of the time I thought I could do anything better than they could (and most of the time I could). This made me strong, it made me masculine and it made me feel invincible.

And, after over twenty years together, I knew that even though Mr Beige was a wonderful man, we weren't meant to be together. Although we still did everything as a married couple, we were really just good friends and an awesome business team. We loved each other but we weren't 'in love'. By the end of our relationship, we hadn't slept together for years, which left me feeling like a man. I felt asexual.

It hurt that I had so much love to give but I didn't feel I could channel my love in the way that I longed to. I also knew if I stayed where I was, I would never experience true love and the gift of children. I needed to find what I was missing. My life and my priorities had to change.

Mr Big

I've always learnt a lot from Mr Big. Mr Big is masculine, self-assured and confident. He would never feel threatened by a woman's success. He's had life experiences and he always has a huge vision. It's so easy to be feminine around him. Being so strong, he creates polarity. He always makes sure he looks after those close to him.

Interestingly, we first met ten years prior to us becoming friends. We didn't really like each other back then – I was very masculine and he was a total alpha male who didn't really think about anyone outside of himself. However, after I realised that I had strong masculine energy and he realised there were other people in the world besides him, we became good friends. (He likes to say that I was a bitch, but that was just my masculine energy butting with his.)

We became friends after I had a number of realisations. I realised that I could be vulnerable with him and I could be smart. I never had to 'dumb myself down' as I always felt I had to with other men. I could drop my barriers. I felt safe.

What's he like? Mr Big is fun, spontaneous and adventurous. He is a pilot and has planes and boats. He has multiple overseas businesses, travels in limousines, stays at the best hotels, dines at the finest restaurants and has connections to extremely powerful people all over the world. Since being in my life, he's been my rock. When my parents died, I was sad and fearful for so many reasons. Mr Big said, 'It's okay. Don't worry – I will always have your back.' His words made me feel better; he made me feel like I wasn't alone.

Since knowing him, he has not only been my rock, he has also been my knight in shining armour. When I'm upset or worried, he always knows how to make me feel better. Sometimes it only takes a few words or a hug. We know how to make each other feel better and we know how to make each other laugh.

I love Mr Big and I also love the fact that I'm not dependent on him for my happiness. I am grateful that I have the strength, inner peace and confidence in myself to be happy with me first and foremost.

I know without a doubt that if I had stayed in my masculine energy, we could never have had the connection and the friendship we have. Our energy would not have allowed it. I feel an amazing sense of gratitude every day for having him in my life.

It's time to meet your white knight

When you were a little girl, do you remember how much you loved fairy tales? You fantasised that a prince was going to ride into town; he would make you his princess and you would live with him in his castle, happily ever after.

I guess we can say that it does happen; it happened with Mary, Crown Princess of Denmark. Princess Mary met Frederik, Crown Prince of Denmark at The Slip Inn, a hotel in Sydney, when the prince was visiting Australia during the 2000 Summer Olympics. This is the classic fairy tale of a commoner marrying royalty.

As women, sometimes we feel that we need to be all things to all people. A brilliant wife, mother, sister, business owner, employee, friend, adviser, counsellor, you name it. We feel we must try and fix everyone, help anyone who needs us and, at the same time, we want to save the world. It can be tiring and overwhelming trying to juggle dozens of balls.

In reality, in order to save the world, we must first save ourselves. At other times, we must allow ourselves to be saved. Sometimes people do come to the rescue – sometimes when you least expect it, and sometimes those you least expect. The universe has a wonderful way of taking care of us.

You can still have the business or high-powered career while attracting a man with whom you can have a passionate, lifelong romance.

You can have everything you want. The world is your oyster.

After reading *Banish the Bitch and Bring Out the Babe*, you may not find your prince. However, if you are ready, you will have the tools you need to find your knight in shining armour.

Before we start

A big part of being in your feminine energy is to *feel* your emotions. Because of this, I'm going to ask you to do something a little different to the normal way we read books. You are not only going to *read* this book, you are going to *actively participate* in learning and *feel* as you read.

Throughout this book, at certain points, I want you to experience what it feels like to be in either your masculine or feminine energy.

In NLP, what we are going to do is known as anchoring.

An anchor is a feeling you associate with something or someone, kind of like Pavlov's dogs. In the 1890s, a Russian physiologist called Pavlov ran experiments to test conditioned responses to situations, in this case, dogs salivating in response to being fed. Initially, Pavlov rang a bell as dogs were given food. After repeating this a number of times, he started ringing the bell in isolation, which triggered the same response. The dogs developed an anchor to the bell.

In the first few chapters of this book, I've created something similar for you. (Don't worry – I won't make you dribble.)

While reading this book, you are going to form positive anchors that will allow you to access the feelings of each energy. As these anchors become stronger, they will become a metaphorical on/off switch for your masculine and feminine energy.

In the beginning, this may feel strange and foreign. You may think you are doing it incorrectly. Don't worry – many of us will feel this way.

However, the more you practise and play with it, the better you will feel. Repetition is how you will master the skill.

So, how do you do this?

You are going to use your left and right fists as your anchors.

There is a theory that the left side of the brain controls the right-hand side of the body and the right side of the brain controls the left-hand side of the body.

The left side of the brain is masculine. When someone is known to be left-brained, (masculine) they tend to be practical, motivated, analytical and driven. The left side of the brain is associated with aggression, physical strength, control and ego.

The right side of the brain is feminine. Those who are right-brained (feminine) are creative, sensitive, nurturing and easy-going. The right brain is associated with creativity, inner strength and intuition.

The left side of the body is feminine.

The right side of the body is masculine. Is it a coincidence that I tend to feel all of my stress in my shoulder on the right side of my body?

You're going to take advantage of this theory when reading this book.

As you read through, I will ask you to feel what it's like to feel feminine and what it feels like to feel masculine, we will use the following symbols:

♂ I will use this symbol when you need to access your masculine anchor and connect to your masculine energy.

♀ And this symbol when you need to access your feminine anchor and connect to your feminine energy.

As you are reading, when I ask you to access your feminine anchor, I want you to squeeze your left fist. When I talk about your masculine anchor, I want you to squeeze your right fist. Really connect to your feminine or masculine energy. You will then always carry those feelings in the palm of your hand, and you can access them when you need to by simply squeezing your left or right fist.

Another option is using one of our *Banish the Bitch* bracelets, available at http://banishthebitch.com/bracelet/, as your anchor. For a demonstration on how to use these anchors, please go to our website.

There are different styles available in our online store, depending on what resonates with you. We have reversible bracelets where one side is pink (feminine) and the flip side is blue (masculine). There are many other styles to choose from.

If you have our reversible bracelet, wear it on your left hand with the feminine side facing out as instructed as you're reading about feminine energy. When you're reading about masculine energy, flip it to the masculine side and wear it on your right hand. Your bracelet will become something to use as a reminder – like an on/off switch for your energies. Then you can flick it over to masculine energy or feminine energy as required.

If you have our single-sided wristband, you can wear the bracelet on your left hand when you are in your feminine and you can flick the switch and swap it to your right hand when you are in your masculine energy.

And shhhh! This is secret women's business. When you purchase a *Banish the Bitch* bracelet, don't tell the men in your life what the bracelet is or what it does.

If you have a disagreement about something with your man, you don't want him to say negative things about your bracelet, like, 'You're being a bitch – turn over your bracelet.' It's yours to use for you, not his to use against you.

Part 1

All about you

Chapter 1: Feminine energy

A girl knows her limits but a wise girl knows she has none.

— Marilyn Monroe

In 2003, I was single and I was on a mission to find out what it meant to be feminine. On my quest to find out what masculine energy looked like, I asked a friend of mine, Mark, if he thought I was masculine. I couldn't believe it when he said, 'Yes'!

Grrrrrrrr...

He apologised once he saw the look on my face. 'I'm sorry, I didn't realise you were so sensitive.'

'I'm not,' I shot back, before realising that I was very sensitive. It hurt to think that someone thought I was masculine. I'd been trying so hard to be feminine.

When I asked him what being feminine meant, he threw the question straight back to me. 'What do you think being feminine is?'

'Oh God, I don't know... to be free?' I had *no freaking idea*.

I asked plenty of other men around the same time if they thought I was masculine, and the answer was always the same.

I thought, 'That's it, I'm going to cry.' (But I didn't cry – I was *way* too masculine for that.) I instead decided to make it my mission to discover more about becoming feminine.

I had felt like I was a man for so long that I really had no idea what being feminine was like. I was so good at concealing my emotions that I had unknowingly erected a thousand barriers between me, my emotions and everyone else. There was no way that I would have let myself cry. I never shared the pain I was feeling and I never shared my problems. I just dealt with them. I was a machine, a robot, going through life's motions.

Now, it's a different story. I feel in touch with my emotions and I share them with others around me. I feel more connected to myself and others. I also feel feminine.

What is feminine energy?

As discussed in the Introduction, we have two types of energy in our relationships and in our own bodies – masculine and feminine energy. At a very high level, masculine energy is strong, focused, driven and controlling, while feminine energy is soft, free-flowing, adventurous and open. In this chapter, I'll be focusing on how you feel in feminine energy and what it looks like to you and to others.

When you are comfortable in your feminine energy, you have faith and trust, and you allow yourself to be vulnerable. Because of this trust, you don't feel the need to control everything – you know you're supported and that everything will be taken care of. Whether it's a man choosing a restaurant, a driving route or a holiday, you are comfortable letting him take care of it (and you!).

In your feminine energy, you are playful, fun and carefree. You grow and thrive on attention and are driven by love and connection. Feeling like you're part of a family unit, or having a 'nest' (your home) where you can focus and direct your love, makes you feel stable and certain.

The key trait of feminine energy is that you enjoy *being*, rather than focusing on everything that needs to get done. You are in the moment. You have the ability to appreciate the colours around you; you appreciate the birds and the flowers. By being in the moment, you have the ability to connect with nature. You have a certain kind

Chapter 1: Feminine energy

of peace. Beyond seeing the surface-level things around you, you begin to *feel* them.

When you're in your feminine energy, you'll find you get out of your head and go into your heart.

~ What masculine men say ~

Mark said that when he's attracted to a woman across a crowded room, this is what she looks like: She's in her own world, she has a big smile on her face, she's comfortable in her own skin, laughing and talking. He said that in itself was a turn-on.

Feminine energy is always flowing, and you'll find that you flow too when you're in your feminine energy. One minute you could be thinking about your children, then your family and then your partner. Sometimes it might even drive you nuts!

To feel certain, however, the feminine needs to feel balanced. When she doesn't feel like she has balance, she can begin to look for ways to create that support and certainty for herself. Whether she is with a man or single, if she doesn't find the balance of a man's masculine energy if she needs to, she may adapt and become the masculine energy herself. This often comes at the cost of losing her feminine energy. She will find herself taking control of everything, making all the decisions and focusing on *doing* rather than *being*, mainly because she doesn't trust that she is taken care of.

This throws her energy out of balance.

Feminine energy can be very unpredictable in her moods, emotions and actions. She can make simple things complicated – because she naturally takes everything into account, she can overthink things to the extreme.

Those in their feminine energy also have a tendency to focus on helping others and can be incredibly giving and unselfish, so much so that they neglect themselves. They can put other people's needs ahead of their own.

Banish The Bitch And Bring Out The Babe

Another way women neglect themselves is when they put their lives on hold for the men they love. An uncertain relationship can leave a woman feeling paralysed and unsettled. She can feel paralysed because she can't see a future with her man or a future without him. She feels stuck. When the feminine is in a relationship with the strong, balanced masculine, she'll feel safe, certain and free to be herself.

The feminine can get obsessed with what <u>could</u> be and what <u>might</u> be in a relationship, not necessarily what's real.

How feminine energy *feels*

When I'm in my feminine energy, I am myself. I'm present. I'm aware of the birds chirping, the sun on my face and how I'm feeling. I'm aware of how others are feeling. I don't have barriers or walls placed around me so that no one can get to know the real me. I am open and I am real. I am vulnerable.

I trust. I trust that everything happens for a reason. I have faith that everything will work out exactly as it should. I know that I am guided and protected.

I am free. I can laugh and dance and sing. I'm open to new things. I feel my energy flowing. I feel free to be myself. I'm free to let my man, my family, my friends and the universe protect and guide me.

I feel centred and happy. I cry when I'm upset and I cry when I'm really happy. I let all of my emotions run through me as I feel them. I don't hold anything in.

I'm smart and I don't allow people to take advantage of me. I'm also vulnerable at the same time. I share my inner feelings with my friends.

I love everyone and I know that they are doing the best with the resources they have. I don't judge anyone – I want everyone to be happy. I see everyone as individuals who have the same needs and desires as me. I see that sometimes people are scared just like I am. I love to take care of people and make sure they are happy. I don't like

Chapter 1: Feminine energy

to see anyone in pain or hurting. I like to think that I can cheer people up and help them to feel better.

I love myself. I appreciate my body and my beauty.

When I am feminine, I *be*.

~ What feminine women say ~

The power of my feminine energy comes from a feeling that is ingrained in my heart. It is certainty and freedom at the same time. It is being assertive with love and caring while wearing a smile. It is a radiance that comes from within my soul and shines upon everyone I come in contact with. It's courage, faith and flowing energy that provides me with the strength to influence with grace and elegance.

– Laurie

What feminine energy *isn't*

I once attended an Anthony Robbins event where we were asked to put on a visual demonstration of masculine and feminine energy. Women who considered themselves to be feminine were asked to dance on the stage, and the audience had to vote whom they thought was the most feminine.

Interestingly, many of the girls started doing very suggestive, sexualised moves, and were surprised when they did not get voted as being the most feminine. Instead, the girls who danced for themselves, who were free and happy, were the ones that were voted as being the most feminine.

Feminine energy isn't about being overtly sexual or trying to lure a man in. It's about enjoying your beauty and sensuality for *you*. Trying to be sexy from a place of needing or wanting a man to complete you is not sexy; that is masculine behaviour. It comes across as promiscuous, and is more likely to lead to a one-night stand than a relationship. Loving who you are and enjoying being in your body is sexy, and will naturally draw in masculine men who would love to learn more about you.

> *There is more to sex appeal than just measurements. I don't need a bedroom to prove my womanliness. I can convey just as much sex appeal picking apples off a tree or standing in the rain.*
>
> – Audrey Hepburn

How will adopting feminine energy enhance your life?

- Once you can master how feminine energy feels, you will experience less stress as you let go of feeling the need to do everything.
- You won't be so stressed anymore as you won't be trying to control everything and everyone.
- You will have more energy because you aren't constantly switched on – you will allow yourself to relax.
- You will create the opportunity to be able to feel love with someone at the deepest level and feel that love reciprocated. If you don't allow yourself to feel love, all you may ever experience are the material trappings of success. You may never feel anything of substance or depth. Don't get me wrong, you can be successful and feel happy to a certain point. However, without love, you can also feel incredibly lonely.
- You will be more likely to attract a strong man, as he sees a space he can fill, while very masculine women may give off the impression they don't need a man.

- You will become more vibrant, sensual, happy and playful, all of which attract men, giving you the power to choose the right one for you.
- You will be able to recognise feminine qualities in yourself and others, which gives you the power to enhance your feminine traits.
- Your friends will get to know the real you, not the guarded person they once knew.
- You will understand and connect with other feminine women and relate to them on a deeper level.
- You will learn how to spot a feminine man *before* you get involved in a relationship with one. It will also help you identify masculine men.

On the other hand, if you *don't* find your feminine energy...

- If you keep going full speed in your masculine energy, you will risk burn-out because you are trying to do everything yourself.
- If you don't allow your heart to open and be vulnerable, you could experience periods of loneliness and a lack of connection with others, simply because you never let anyone get to know the *real* you.
- You may never find your Mr Right.

Why do we resist feminine energy?

Even though feminine energy is very powerful, many modern women resist their femininity. Some see feminine women as ditsy or dumb, others worry about attracting too much attention from men, and others hate the idea of being weak.

What you'll soon discover is that most of these fears have more to do with our perceptions than the reality of true femininity.

'Being feminine is being ditsy'

When I was in my masculine energy, I thought that being feminine meant you were weak or ditsy.

A few years ago, I went on a weekend away and I met a lady who was feminine to the extreme. She was single and her main focus in life was peace and love. Her beliefs were that it was bad to make money, and any money she did make she had to give away to help others. Because of this, she struggled financially and people took advantage of her.

She had no power in her life. She was like a ship without a rudder – being blown around with no direction. She looked helpless. She looked like she needed someone to save her.

I looked at 'feminine' women like her and thought: Why would I want to surrender my power? Why would I want to appear weak or ditsy? Why would I ever want to put myself in a compromising position?

Now I understand that she was extremely feminine. She put everyone's needs ahead of her own. She forgot to take care of herself. She needed to adopt some masculine energy to balance herself.

Being feminine does not mean you are weak, nor is it ditsy or dumb, though sometimes women surrender control to the extent where they allow others to make bad decisions on their behalf. Some of us allow our men to step up in all areas and we take a back seat. We allow them to make bad decisions without us taking ownership or assuming control. If a bad decision is in the process of being made and it involves you, you need to speak up and discuss it. You don't want to have things happen you could have avoided. You don't want regrets.

For instance, I read a lot of dating books when I was single, and my understanding of a number of books to do with masculine and feminine energy was that women should surrender all financial decisions to their male partner. Wanting to have and experience the feminine role in my second relationship, I surrendered. It was singularly one of the most stupid decisions I ever made. I ended up much worse off financially and emotionally for it. In the relationship, I was much better at managing money. I should have managed it. I didn't.

Chapter 1: Feminine energy

An integrated woman can be feminine and yet still look after herself. She is smart and she takes control where she needs to.

> ### ♀ Anchor to your feminine energy — Connect to your feminine energy.
>
> Clench your left fist and feel every word while you read the section below.
>
> If you have one of our *Banish the Bitch* bracelets, wear it on your left wrist. Feel the bracelet acting as an anchor and allow it to store and remind you of the feelings below.
>
> Breathe deeply and read these words out loud. And allow the words to fill your entire body. Feel them.
>
> *I am feminine.*
>
> *I am smart.*
>
> *I am a good person.*
>
> *I look for the good in everything and everyone.*
>
> *I am loving, honest, caring and open to those I trust.*
>
> *I am a confident and capable woman.*
>
> *I love myself.*
>
> *I do not let other people take advantage of me.*
>
> *I am also a kick-ass bitch when I need to be.*
>
> You have to take care of yourself, your finances and your children (or future children). In nature, a lioness is powerful and feminine. The lion is the leader of the pack and she never challenges him. However, she would never allow herself or her cubs be put in a compromising position. She would not leave them unprotected. Emulate *her* as a role model for masculine and feminine energy.

Banish The Bitch And Bring Out The Babe

> If you need to feel these feelings throughout the day, simply clench your left fist or wear your bracelet on your left wrist to re-establish your anchor.

'I'll get too much attention from men'

Some women figure that if they don't dress in a feminine way – if they don't try to be pretty or if they aren't attractive – they won't have to worry about men.

Some women are worried about being the subject of men's attention. Some believe their level of attractiveness could affect their safety if they are followed home on a dark night. They figure if they are less attractive, they will be safer.

Some young women also find it hard to say 'no' to men. Some don't want to be put in the position of turning down an advance. They don't want to feel uncomfortable and they don't want to hurt the other person's feelings by rejecting them. They would rather not have the advances from men, especially if they don't know how to handle them – they simply don't know what to say.

The truth is, our needs and wants must come first. A strong girl knows what she wants and what she doesn't want; she sets her standards and sets boundaries that she is comfortable with.

We are not being feminine for men. We need to be feminine for us. We need to feel pretty for us. We need to feel feminine for us. We need to be strong when we need to be. With higher self-confidence, we will feel more empowered. We will feel more in control and yet still be able to access our feminine.

We must teach our children to say 'no'. It doesn't matter if we reject a man's advances. If we are not comfortable, we should feel safely able to get out of the situation

Chapter 1: Feminine energy

~ What feminine women say ~

When Lynne was about seventeen, she went on a holiday with her parents. A single man on holiday, twenty-eight-year-old David, had dinner with Lynne and her parents on three or four occasions and, one night, he asked if he could take Lynne out with him to see a band after dinner. Her parents trusted David as they thought he seemed like a decent kind of guy.

He walked her back to her room at midnight and, once they got to her door, he grabbed her and kissed her. She did not know what to do. She found herself in a position she didn't want to be in. She was embarrassed about what to say to him and embarrassed to tell her parents. She wasn't confident enough to say anything.

This is where having self-confidence in your own body kicks in.

From knowing how to set and understand your own boundaries, knowing what you want and don't want, you can tell men in situations such as this that their behaviour is not acceptable.

'Being feminine is being weak'

Feminine women allow themselves to be vulnerable, yet vulnerability isn't a very attractive trait to many powerful, self-sufficient women. When I was in my masculine energy, I thought that vulnerability meant you cried all the time, you were weak and you were dependent. You couldn't do anything yourself and you left yourself exposed by revealing your weaknesses. I actually felt sorry for feminine women.

Today, I see it differently. I see vulnerability as a form of strength (as long as you surrender to the right person). By being open with your man, close friends and family members, you're showing them that you trust them. You are allowing them to feel the deepest form of love and connection, which is a gift to you both. It is powerful. You also allow yourself to let go of the need to constantly control everything and can accept help from others when you need it.

Banish The Bitch And Bring Out The Babe

There is a big difference between being weak and being vulnerable. A balanced, confident, feminine woman isn't weak; she will *not* allow someone to walk all over her. She stands up for herself. She won't allow herself to be a doormat. However, she also doesn't feel the need to fight the world all on her own – after all, that's a lonely place to be. She knows that she can move Heaven and Earth if she needs to, and she also knows that she can ask people to help her. She lets those people into her heart.

By contrast, a weak person (which can be masculine or feminine) just accepts the circumstances around them, even if they could hurt them. Danni, for example, was sent a bill from her telephone company for $700. Prior to this, her normal bill was $100 a month, and she switched plans after the phone company told her she would save money on the new plan. Ultimately, they gave her wrong information, which cost Danni $600 a month. Even though it was wrong and she should never have been billed that amount, Danni opted to pay the account as she did not want to cause trouble.

Weak people are 'yes people' who will say 'yes' to virtually anything to avoid upsetting anyone. Others will often take advantage of them.

Being weak and being vulnerable are two different things.

If someone is normally strong and they're feeling tired, stressed or overwhelmed, if they are put in a similar situation to the one in the phone example, instead of fighting the situation, they may just pay the bill. They may feel that paying it will ease the situation and ease their stress levels. They may be happy that at least they can cross something off their 'to do' list. If you are feeling this way, turn to your support network for strength.

~ What masculine men say ~

Daniel from New York said he's more attracted to a woman when she's vulnerable and open. When he meets a woman, he wants to know what she's like as a person; he wants to know her hopes, her fears and her dreams.

Chapter 1: Feminine energy

He said that, instead of a woman telling him what she's achieved, he finds it much more attractive when she's vulnerable and she lets down her barriers. He doesn't like it when women focus on their achievements and the material things they own. It's competitive.

How do you step into your feminine energy?

To embrace your femininity, all you really need to do is go into your heart. Relax and take big, deep breaths. Feel the love in your heart and connect to your senses.

Feel grateful for every little thing and everyone you have in your life.

> ### ♀ Anchor to your feminine energy – Connect to your feminine energy.
>
> Clench your left fist. Feel every word whilst you read the section below.
>
> If you have one of our *Banish The Bitch* bracelets, wear it on your left wrist. Feel the bracelet acting as an anchor and allow it to store and remind you of the feelings below.
>
> If you need to feel these feelings throughout the day, simply clench your left fist or wear your bracelet on your left wrist to re-establish your anchor.
>
> You are going to take a step into your feminine energy.
>
> To really associate to this process, go to a quiet place outside if you can.
>
> First, take a breath and go into your heart. Take a few minutes and begin to notice your surroundings – the sky, the trees, the roses... Feel what it's like to be a part of nature. Feel the hot sun, feel the cold air...

Banish The Bitch And Bring Out The Babe

> Appreciate everything you have. Be grateful for wherever you are and remember you. Close your eyes for a little while, breathe and feel. Be in the moment.
>
> Feel gratitude for everything you have achieved, no matter how small it may be.
>
> Take another deep breath and exhale slowly. Let go of everything. Notice what you see, hear, feel and smell. Smile and feel loved. Love yourself.
>
> Make a promise to yourself that you will laugh more, live more and love more, and take action every day.

When I was in my masculine stage, I devoted my whole life to the business and never stopped to smell the roses or to enjoy life. When I had a day off work, I didn't know what to do with myself. I would end up working or reading a business book! If you are like I used to be and you don't know how to tap into your feminine energy, here are some ideas:

- Watch a chick flick like *Dirty Dancing* or *Secrets of the Ya Ya Sisterhood*.
- Sing karaoke.
- Go for a massage or meditate.
- Dance around the house.
- Spend time with your feminine girlfriends.
- Be spontaneous – do something you wouldn't normally do.
- Sit on the beach and read a book.
- Connect to nature – watch a sunrise or sunset. Take your shoes off and feel the sand, the dirt, the water or the grass between your toes.
- Go for a kayak.

Chapter 1: Feminine energy

- Listen to nice music and light lots of scented candles around the house.
- Put pictures of friends, family and people you love around the house.
- Make where you live prettier – buy some flowers, candles, matching picture frames, artwork … anything to make it more girly and pretty.
- Write in a journal.
- Read a nice romance novel, or a gossip magazine.
- Hang around masculine men.
- Have a bubble bath with candles and a mud-pack.
- Do some of the feminine anchor exercises that appear throughout this book.
- Organise a dinner party for friends (don't forget to decorate the whole house!).
- Have a date night with your partner.
- Surrender sexually to your partner.
- Go shopping – have a whole day where you spoil yourself.
- Go horseback riding or roller-skating – enjoy something you did as a child.
- Drive a convertible with the top down in a hot outfit!

Over the coming pages, I'll also share some more detailed ideas and practices to help you tap further into your feminine energy.

~ What masculine men say ~

John from Victoria defined femininity as a woman who is totally comfortable within herself and comes from her heart. She gives to herself first, then she has an abundance of love for others. He said that when women give to others but not to themselves, they can look tired and worn out.

Find a role model

If someone else can do something, so can you. Yet, is it any wonder that so many of us get stuck in a masculine role when so many of our role models are strong businessmen? My gurus were Zig Ziglar, Dale Carnegie, Anthony Robbins and Brian Tracy. They were fantastic role models in many areas – business, communication and mindset being just a few – but femininity wasn't one of them.

To model someone, instead think about who you consider to be a successful, integrated woman. Personally, I love Sarah Jessica Parker, Lady Diana, Oprah Winfrey, Jackie Kennedy, Lucille Ball, Goldie Hawn, Audrey Hepburn, Brigitte Bardot, Marilyn Monroe and Grace Kelly. These are examples of smart women with beautiful style and incredible class.

If you are confronted with a situation and you aren't sure what to do, or you feel yourself getting out of balance, just ask yourself, 'What would my role model do?'

What would Jackie Kennedy do?

What would Oprah do?

Look feminine on the outside

Years ago, when I was on a mission to research the differences between masculine and feminine energy, I met Alec from Greece at a self-development seminar. When I asked him if he thought I was masculine, he said that I had masculine mannerisms on the outside, but he knew that I was mush on the inside.

Hmm... I asked him to tell me more.

He said as soon as we met, I went into my masculine energy:

- 💗 I shook hands with him.
- 💗 I made direct eye contact with him to the point it could have felt intimidating

- I told him all about myself and my businesses.
- I was quick with my comments.
- I stood with my arms folded.
- I seemed confrontational.

He said that the way I stood with my arms folded, it looked like I was protecting myself. It made me look like I was independent and closed off to relationships, even friendships. He felt that I was putting out signals I didn't want anyone to come near me.

I then asked Alec what feminine energy looked like to him. He said it was free-flowing and vulnerable. A woman in her feminine energy would have a smile, a soft face and soft eyes. He said that a feminine woman plays with her hair, laughs and there's a certain way that she stands. Her demeanour is welcoming, open and carefree.

After this feedback, I felt very self-conscious about talking about my successes, as Alec said that when a woman continually emphasises how much she has achieved in her career or life to a potential date, it can feel like she's trying to make herself look more successful and more significant than her potential suitor. Alec said that he's okay with his woman being successful and having a strong vision, as long as she doesn't make it a competition between them. He doesn't want to feel like he's competing with his partner.

Men don't care what you have achieved. They want to get to know you.

Being a masculine man, Alec said that he gets so directed and focused on what he's doing and where he's going that sometimes he doesn't see a lot of the things around him. Because of this, it's the simple things that mean the most. He remembers the first time he drove in a car with a lady he was seeing and she put her hand on his shoulder. He loved it as it made her a part of his journey. She connected with him and she got into his focused world. Before she did this, he was purely focused on getting from A to B.

Banish The Bitch And Bring Out The Babe

When embracing your femininity, it starts from within. Beauty isn't about how you look on the outside; it's about what's on the inside. However, looking feminine on the outside can be a reminder that helps you feel more feminine on the inside. So what can you do?

I asked my friend Mark, who worked in the beauty industry, about how I could look more feminine. (In hindsight, I probably should have asked a feminine woman, but he helped me a lot.) He told me to replace my glasses with contact lenses, to get my eyebrows shaped and to grow my hair longer, get it layered and put highlights in it. He then said I might look and feel more feminine if I lost a little weight. I took his recommendations and I felt so much more attractive on the outside.

Are you happy with the way you look? Don't be afraid to ask people you trust what you can do to look more feminine. Choose someone who is fashion conscious and who always looks nice – someone whose opinion you respect. Ask them to tell you honestly how you could improve your appearance. Then, don't be upset when they tell you, because you asked for it! Take everything with a grain of salt, but remember that if a couple of people say it, it's probably a valid point.

Some ideas to get you started:

- Learn which colours suit you and wear them.
- Know your body shape and wear clothing to suit.
- Wear dresses, accessorised with beautiful handbags and jewellery.
- Wear figure-hugging clothes with high-heeled shoes, boots or sexy shoes.
- Wear sexy lingerie – stick your chest out with a push-up or padded bra!
- Learn how to put your makeup on to suit your eyes and your features.

Chapter 1: Feminine energy

- Get a manicure and pedicure.
- Get a Brazilian.
- Try different hairstyles.
- Smile, laugh and have fun.
- Spend time getting ready – go to a bit of extra effort with your makeup and lipstick.
- Put a colour in your hair or grow it long.
- Get rid of any unwanted body hair – wax your top lip and get your eyebrows shaped.
- Wear pink or bright colours as a visual anchor to be feminine.
- Show a little bit of cleavage (but not too much).
- Take care of your health – don't smoke, get enough sleep and eat nourishing food.
- Speak and act like a lady.
- Wear nice perfume.

Feminine clothes

There is a difference between masculine clothes, feminine clothes and sexy clothes. Dressing provocatively is masculine, and can be seen as manipulative. Dressing sexily is feminine and attractive. There is a difference.

To really understand the difference, start to analyse women's fashion magazines. Pay attention to who looks pretty and feminine, who looks sexy, who looks like they are trying too hard and who looks masculine.

Banish The Bitch And Bring Out The Babe

Why do women want to dress like men when they're fortunate enough to be women? Why lose femininity, which is one of our greatest charms? We get more accomplished by being charming than we would be flaunting around in pants and smoking. I'm very fond of men. I think they are wonderful creatures. I love them dearly. But I don't want to look like one. When women gave up their long skirts, they made a grave error...

– Tasha Tudor

Act like a feminine woman

When you flick the switch to your feminine energy, it might take a bit of practice for it to really feel comfortable. Talk to your friends and open up. Talk to men. Practise being feminine.

This doesn't mean acting like a dog on heat – you're not going out to look at every man like you want them. Everyone will see it. Instead, smile and be comfortable in yourself. When men see that you are comfortable in your own skin, they say it's the sexiest thing ever! Look relaxed and approachable.

On the flip side, make sure that you're not sending signals that say you're not interested. You *want* them to talk to you. Men will love you for your spontaneity and your spirit.

Don't be a woman that needs a man; be a woman that a man needs.

Chapter 1: Feminine energy

♀ Anchor to your feminine energy – Connect to your feminine energy.

Clench your left fist. Feel every word whilst you read the section below.

If you have one of our *Banish The Bitch* bracelets, wear it on your left wrist. Feel the bracelet acting as an anchor and allow it to store and remind you of the feelings below.

If you need to feel these feelings throughout the day, simply clench your left fist or wear your bracelet on your left wrist to re-establish your anchor.

Read the points below and imagine that you are every part this feminine woman. Imagine how you would feel being this woman. Feel how it would feel to be free, happy and not judged by anyone, not even yourself.

This is you.

- 💗 You are relaxed enough to laugh (a lot).
- 💗 You are open to talking and you make others feel comfortable.
- 💗 You have no tension in your body. You let your body move.
- 💗 You walk slowly, taking your time.
- 💗 You are comfortable hugging people you love. You are not afraid of physical touch.
- 💗 Your face is soft and your smiles are big.
- 💗 You are confident.
- 💗 You breathe into your heart.

Banish The Bitch And Bring Out The Babe

- When you sit, your ankles are crossed with your legs folded in front of you on an angle. Your head tilts to the side slightly, your arms are soft and your shoulders are back but soft.
- You walk with one foot in front of the other, like models do (try it – it will make you feel sexy!).
- When speaking to people, you stand side on – you're not confronting.
- Your shoulders are back and you move your hips from side to side when you walk.
- You don't scan the room to see who's checking you out; you are comfortable in your own skin.

Feel your emotions

What influenced you as a child?

Did someone tell you not to throw a ball like a girl? When you cried, where you told to stop crying like a little girl?

I remember thinking that I didn't want to cry like that. It made me believe that acting like a girl or showing my emotions was wrong and weak. No wonder we don't want to let our emotions out when we get older.

The truth is that feeling your emotions is natural and feminine.

Expect there to be times when you feel like you need a good cry. That's part of being feminine. It's completely normal to feel happy and centred one minute and then disturbed or upset the next. Men don't understand this. I didn't really understand it either, until I found out it happened to just about every woman in the world. Most women think that it's only happening to them. It's a great discovery and a great feeling when you find out you're not alone, that you're normal.

Chapter 1: Feminine energy

Why do we feel this way?

Feminine energy stores emotions. When we talk to our friends or family and we hear their pain, we feel it. We empathise. We have our own emotions and we take on everyone else's too.

What do we do if we feel overcome with emotion?

We feel sad, cranky or upset – we feel all the emotions under the sun.

When we release our emotions, it allows us to feel normal again.

You can have a good cry, go for a run or a swim, make love, hit a punching bag or scream into a pillow. Have a long bath and listen to your favourite music. Talk to your girlfriends and vent. You can journal your feelings to really get to the bottom of why you are feeling the way you are feeling.

You need to release your built-up feelings in whatever way works for you.

> *Women need real moments of solitude and self-reflection to balance out how much of ourselves we give away.*
>
> – Margaret Thatcher.

Accept help, gifts and compliments

Sometimes people want to help. It's that simple.

I remember a while back, a business associate asked me out for lunch. I had to leave early, so on the way out I settled the bill. When I got back to work, he called me, quite perturbed. He said that I had insulted him. He explained that he asked me out to lunch because he wanted to thank me for some of the work deals we had achieved together. By paying, I didn't let him express his gratitude. I had unintentionally insulted him.

Banish The Bitch And Bring Out The Babe

The universe is a magical place and it can deliver lots of surprises and opportunities. Gifts and help can come in many forms. Feminine women are open to receiving. If you keep pushing help away, help might stop coming to you.

As strong women, sometimes we deny men the gift of treating us, or helping us. As strong women, sometimes we make sure that we let everyone know that we are independent and, in doing so, we reject others. Sometimes we think that if we accept the gift, we'll be obligated to the other person or we will owe them.

When we empower ourselves and we practise self-love, self-acceptance and self-esteem, this becomes less of an issue. When you're not worried about what other people will think of you, you can be open to trusting and you can be vulnerable. When you are truly in your own body, then you can accept people helping you.

Please let others take care of you sometimes. Allow yourself to be in the position where you can say 'thank you' with a smile.

The same goes for accepting the gift of compliments. Have you ever told someone they look nice and they argued with you? How did it make you feel? Accept compliments, especially from men. People wouldn't say you looked nice if you didn't. Get used to saying 'thank you'.

Eventually, it will become natural.

~ What masculine men say ~

Mark told me about when he met his future wife at a party some years back. He said that when she walked in to the room, she lit up the room. She was bubbly, feminine, happy and fun. They talked for hours about all kinds of things and they spoke about how they felt being single. She said something along the lines of, 'Some days I get really lonely... Some days I feel like I'm just not getting anywhere.' As she was telling him this, he said he just felt like he wanted to help her. He felt he could fill the gaps. He knew he could make her happy. He was attracted to her femininity and her vulnerability.

Chapter 1: Feminine energy

♀︎ Anchor to feminine energy – Connect to your feminine energy.

Clench your left fist. Feel every word whilst you read the section below.

If you have one of our *Banish The Bitch* bracelets, wear it on your left wrist. Feel the bracelet acting as an anchor and allow it to store and remind you of the feelings below.

If you need to feel these feelings throughout the day, simply clench your left fist or wear your bracelet on your left wrist to re-establish your anchor.

Imagine saying 'yes' to the following scenarios. Feel what it would be like.

Know that it's okay to say 'yes' to:

- Compliments – Someone says that your dress looks nice or your hair looks nice. Your response – Say thank you.
- Help – Someone offers to give you some money when you are short on funds. Your response – Say thank you.
- Being vulnerable – You visit a close girlfriend that you trust and you share how you really feel. You are honest and open.
- Letting a man take care of you – You are asked out to dinner by a man you really like and he wants to pay. Your response – Say yes and say thank you.
- Allowing yourself to feel love and feel happy – Breathe into your heart, feel love and feel peace. Accept love.
- Having faith that things will work out – Don't worry about EVERYTHING.

Banish The Bitch And Bring Out The Babe

- Relaxing – Imagine you are either at the beach in the sun with a great book, or in the bush with a big, beautiful fire burning. Enjoy the moment.

- Letting go and releasing your need to control. Don't hold on to things so tightly. Imagine not fighting every battle, when someone says something that you don't agree with. Let it go. Relax.

In each of these situations, feel what it would feel like to feel those feelings. Feel what it would feel like not to be so stressed all the time.

Summary

If only I knew then what I know now...

- At the most basic level, feminine energy is about *being* while masculine energy is about *doing*.

- Feminine energy allows you to open your heart to feeling love at the deepest level. If you don't allow yourself to feel love, all you may ever experience is the token trophies or material bells and whistles of life and relationships. You may only feel surface happiness.

- Many modern women resist being feminine, because they see it as being ditsy, promiscuous or weak.

Chapter 1: Feminine energy

- Becoming more feminine will help you attract a masculine man. It will also encourage the right men in your life to step up and become more masculine.
- Feeling all the emotions in the world is normal for a woman.
- To tap into your feminine energy, look feminine on the outside, act feminine, feel your emotions and accept gifts. These outside actions will help you feel more feminine on the inside too.

Exercises

1. Embrace your femininity. Practise getting out of your head and going into your heart. Close your eyes, relax and take big, deep breaths. Feel love in your heart and connect to wherever you are and whomever you are with. Be in the moment. Feel absolute gratitude for everything you have had and everything you currently have in your life.

2. Connect to nature. Go for a walk on the beach or in the bush and feel the sand or dirt on your feet. Feel the sun and wind on your face. Make a special effort to watch a sunrise or sunset. Connect to earth.

3. Get to know people from your heart. Drop any barriers you have and speak from your heart. Practise this first with people you trust. You will notice that others will feel connected to your feminine energy very quickly. In your feminine energy, you are genuine and open. You make others feel comfortable as they don't detect any selfishness or any ulterior motives. You will probably begin to find that people will tell you things that they would never normally share with others. They will feel comfortable with you.

Chapter 2: Masculine energy

> *Masculinity is not something given to you, but something you gain. And you gain it by winning small battles with honour.*
>
> – Norman Mailer

What is masculine energy?

Adopting masculine energy gives a woman confidence and the determination to make things happen. When you feel like giving up, you will have a voice inside you that says, 'Suck it up, princess.' Unlike feminine energy, masculine energy focuses on the head, not the heart. This energy is logical and practical.

Those who are firmly balanced in their masculine energy are centred, strong and unshakable, like an old oak tree. They are focused, driven, disciplined and determined. They are in control. They do what they say they will.

The masculine thrive on a clear sense of purpose. It's their reason for living. Those in their masculine energy are at their best when they have a big picture in mind for what they want to achieve. When someone tries to take them away from that vision, they do not tolerate it. They become like a speeding train – unstoppable.

They love to finish projects and they aim to finish what they start. It's then that they can experience peace … for a little while, at least.

The danger is that, when out of balance, masculine energy can lead you to make work the most important thing in your life. It can start to fill your needs more than anything else in the world, which is why feminine energy is important to create balance and to fill the obvious gaps.

When I was running my business and my personal life on masculine energy, I felt driven, disciplined and focused to the point of obsession. If I wasn't working, I was reading a book about work – I literally didn't stop. I tried to stay in control of everything and everyone. I had plenty of cash in the bank and went on lots of awesome holidays. I was, by anyone's standards, successful in my field.

I also found that there were massive trade-offs.

I always had a knot in my stomach. I was always stressed. If I was at work, I was working. If I wasn't at work, I felt terribly guilty that I wasn't. I was stressed, sad, unhappy, guilty and exhausted. I knew that if I kept it up I would die of a stress-related illness. That's how much pressure I felt. I truly wondered if there was something wrong with me.

The pivotal point was when I realised exactly why I was so unhappy – I realised that I was permanently in my masculine energy.

Because those in their masculine energy are so busy thinking about how they will achieve their goals, they rarely take the time to smell the roses. This is where feminine energy can bring some balance – by learning to *be*, they can appreciate a beautiful sunset, flower or animal. This balance helps them to see something they may not have seen in a more focused state of mind.

Being in your masculine energy, you make big things simple. Rather than taking in all the small details, you aim for efficiency, assessing the easiest way to complete a task with minimal effort. You are more clear-cut with solutions to problems. You take calculated risks when appropriate.

Chapter 2: Masculine energy

When you are in your masculine energy, you have a strong sense of self and are comfortable in your own skin. You're proud of the things you've achieved. You could be seen as ego or success-driven and you thrive on a challenge.

In your masculine energy, you put yourself first. This could lead others to see you as selfish, especially when you're on a mission. In order to focus and get things done, you may have to sacrifice time with those close to you.

Masculine energy craves respect and admiration, which can make masculine men and women vulnerable if they don't feel respected or admired by those closest to them. The greatest fears of someone in their masculine energy are not being enough, rejection and not being able to control the situation.

How masculine energy *feels*

When I am in my masculine energy, I am totally confident that I will achieve the results I need. I have my goals, I know my direction and I make myself accountable. I do whatever it takes to get the outcome I need completed. If I need to stay back at work until midnight, I will.

I have an aura about me – I'm unstoppable. I'm focused and directed. I'm determined to get my result. If I need to get help from someone, I will source the help I need.

To the outside world, I am unshakable. I never let anyone know if I have any doubts, or if I am even doubting myself. I'm guarded. Even if I feel nervous or scared of the result, as far as staff and other people are concerned, I never waiver. I always tell them I am confident and everything is going well.

I stand up for what I believe in. I protect myself and those close to me. If I need to tell someone off or chastise someone, I do.

I don't let anyone see my emotions. I don't let myself really feel my emotions either. I get the job done.

I just *do* – simple.

Banish The Bitch And Bring Out The Babe

~ What masculine men say ~

John from Melbourne said it's clear that masculine women operate from their heads and not their hearts. He finds that women who say 'I have this' or 'I have that' are out to impress instead of coming from their heart. He said that men are generally much more attracted to a woman's physical assets, rather than their credentials.

♂ Anchor to your masculine energy – Connect to your masculine energy.

Clench your right fist. Feel every word while you read the section below.

If you have one of our *Banish the Bitch* bracelets, wear it on your right wrist. Feel the bracelet acting as an anchor and allow it to store and remind you of the feelings below.

Masculine energy is embodied by strong, empowered *doing* words. While these are different for each person, below are some examples. Read each word aloud and take a moment to feel the energy of it. Imagine yourself with this strong state of mind.

- Focused – You are focused on what you need to achieve.
- Successful – You have completed a massive task that you were working on.
- Determined – You know you are going to finish a task you have on your list.
- Winning – You have completed a lot of your to do list; you are on track.
- Recognised – You have received an award for your efforts.

- Accomplished – You are great at what you do and you know it.
- Wealthy – You receive financial rewards.
- Significant – You are on top of the world; you feel important.
- Variety – You have a life full of adventure.
- Achievement – You are always taking things to the next level.
- Growth – Each day, you learn and grow.
- Tenacity – You never give up.
- Domination – You either dominate your field or you aim to.

Feel the feelings. These feelings drive masculine energy.

If you need to feel these feelings throughout the day, simply clench your right fist or wear your bracelet on the right wrist to re-establish your anchor.

Why is masculine energy important?

It's important to understand masculine energy for three reasons:

- By understanding masculine energy, you can access those traits in yourself when you need them. You need masculine energy, particularly when life gets tough and you need to stick up for yourself or when you want to achieve massive goals and make things happen. After all, no one wants to be a doormat.

- By understanding masculine energy, you will be able to identify a masculine man before you become involved in a relationship. If you want to be the feminine energy, you will know whom to look for. You will also recognise who the feminine men are so you don't end up choosing them, which could make you the masculine energy in your relationship.

- By understanding how the masculine thinks, you can relate to him better and create a better relationship for both of you. You will not be second-guessing his behaviour. You will understand him so much more.

Why do we resist our masculine energy?

As I mentioned earlier, whenever someone used to say I had masculine energy, I would almost burst into tears! I felt hurt. I was insulted. I felt like it was wrong for me to have masculine energy.

Now I know that's *bullshit* – of course we need both energies.

Masculine energy is important when life gets tough and you need to take care of yourself. Even if you feel like you have nothing left with which to move forward, sometimes you need to harden up, dig deep and give it everything you have. Particularly if your survival depends on it.

However, even though that's the case, a lot of women still have resistance to having masculine energy. Some can be scared of challenging the status quo and going after what they truly want. They are scared of who they think they have to become, or who they may have to push out of the way or tread on, to get where they want to go. Some believe in order to get to the top, you have to do the wrong thing to get there. This is not true.

Chapter 2: Masculine energy

'Masculine energy means being an asshole'

Masculine means you are focused and driven, but just because you have goals and desires it doesn't mean you treat people badly. It also doesn't mean you are taking something from someone else.

Masculine energy, in its pure essence, is not destructive or bad and it doesn't mean you have to be an asshole – especially in relationships.

Balanced masculine energy is centred, loving and nurturing. Remember that there's strength and power in each energy.

'Masculine energy is intimidating'

Strong, independent women who are driven by significance can definitely send a clear message to men. The message is that they don't need a man and that they can do everything by themselves. After all, you're focused, directed and you know what you want. You've set goals and achieved them on many occasions.

When you're successful in this way, you can be intimidating to any man who isn't sure of himself. Some of these men may not have done what you have. They may have no vision, a smaller vision than you or they may not have had as many life experiences as you.

Life experiences can sometimes make it hard to relate to a lot of men, especially if you have experienced highs and lows in your life. You may have run successful businesses, travelled extensively, moved, experienced deaths in your family and had children. You may have many references for things they don't. You may have made many more mistakes and also have more of life's lessons under your belt. It can seem to many men that you've done it all.

When I was young and single, I found myself in this position. Some men would say that they thought it would be hard for me to find a man because other men could find me intimidating.

Now I understand that *they* were the ones who felt intimidated.

You can still call on your masculine energy, follow your vision, do and achieve, especially if this is fulfilling for you. You shouldn't have to dumb yourself down or stop following your dreams to make the men around you comfortable. Instead, the goal should be finding a man who is proud of what you do, who isn't threatened by what you have achieved. This may be a man who has also achieved.

There is a balance to strike between your strong, masculine, achieving energy and your soft, feminine, experiencing energy. The key is not to challenge a man with your achievements. He isn't your competition. There's no reason to communicate that:

- You're smarter than him.
- You're stronger than him.
- You earn more money than him.
- You're more successful than him.
- You're more significant than him.
- You don't need him.
- You're already happy and there is no room for him.
- He has nothing to add to your life.

It's when you give off this competitive energy that a masculine man won't be interested in pursuing a relationship.

How do you transform into masculine energy?

I asked Peter, who is the most masculine man I know, the following question: 'What do you do to FEEL masculine?' He said, 'What do you mean? I just wake up in the morning.' I said, 'No... What do you DO to feel masculine?' He said, 'I don't bloody do anything. I just wake up.' I laughed and then I thought, *Oh, I get it... He just wakes up, scratches himself, passes wind and thinks, 'I'm a man!'*

Chapter 2: Masculine energy

My point is he just FEELS masculine. Once you understand and you anchor both energies in your body, you will feel both energies in your body, anytime you need them.

> ♂ **Anchor to your masculine energy – Connect to your masculine energy.**
>
> Clench your right fist. Feel every word whilst you read the section below.
>
> If you have one of our *Banish The Bitch* bracelets, wear it on your right wrist. Feel the bracelet acting as an anchor and allow it to store and remind you of the feelings below.
>
> If you need to feel these feelings throughout the day, simply clench your right fist or wear your bracelet on your right wrist to re-establish your anchor.
>
> When you need to access your masculine energy, focus all of your thoughts on the actions you are taking rather than your feelings – this way your mind can't get clogged up with your emotions.
>
> In your everyday life in this state, you won't feel what you are doing – you will just do it. You will plan and you will be logical in your decisions. You will be disciplined and you will make things happen.
>
> For the purposes of being associated with masculine energy, with the next exercise I want you to imagine you are feeling what it would be like to be in your masculine energy.
>
> - Get into your head – Focus on your task.
> - Write a 'to do' list and create daily schedules.
> - Set some big daily, weekly, monthly and yearly goals.
> - Be disciplined (you may need a strong accountability partner to keep you on track).

Banish The Bitch And Bring Out The Babe

- Check in on your goals daily (as you do this, also make sure they're aligned with your heart so you are not completely lost in your masculine energy).
- Focus on your end result. Don't see it happening any other way than you planned.
- Stand up for what you believe in.
- Speak straight to the point.
- Have the mindset that you will handle your problems and take care of your business. Map out each thing you have to do, step-by-step.
- Strategise, plan and have a clear vision.
- Get naked in front of your partner – Initiate and take control in a sexual situation with your partner; get on top!
- Ride a motorbike.
- Work in the garden and fix things around the house.
- Be confident.
- Be a leader in your own way.
- Have a strong purpose.
- Fart and laugh at fart jokes. (Well… that's what men do, isn't it?)

If you want to find your masculine power instantly, join a martial arts class.

Now that I get it, I don't care if people say that I have masculine energy. I know it's actually an awesome quality to have. I can be strong when I need to be and then I can switch over to my feminine energy. I can carry off both energies with ease, depending on the situation and where I need to be. I know that everything is in balance.

Chapter 2: Masculine energy

Transitioning between energies

We know that we have masculine and feminine energy; make sure you use both. It can be easy to get lost in one energy; for example, you could get caught up at work and come home in that state. Make sure you get used to flicking your switch and using your anchors of masculine and feminine energy. Consciously flick your switch to either masculine or feminine energy. Use your left or right fist, or use your bracelet. Don't get so lost in one that you forget the other side of yourself.

Some people learn the skill of masculine energy and throw themselves into their masculine by totally immersing themselves in work; they forget to flick their switch so they can smell the roses. Likewise, don't throw yourself into your feminine and quit your job and give up your career. Keep your energy in check.

> *I go feminine, I go masculine. I am both, actually. I think the male side is a bit stronger in me, and I have to tone it down sometimes. I'm not like a normal woman, that's for sure.*
>
> – Grace Jones

Adopt masculine physiology

Study masculine men. Notice how they carry themselves.

A masculine man sits with his shoulders back, his head steady and his eyes focused. He sits with his legs straight out in front, or one foot resting on the other knee. He knows his purpose. He's focused. He's present. He's confident. He's centred. He has the respect of other men (and women).

When he stands, he stands straight on. If he's with another man, he may stand to the side a bit so that he appears non-confrontational.

When he walks, he takes long, confident strides. The movement looks like it's propelled by his shoulders rather than his hips. His arms swing slightly, but not so much that he looks like he's a gorilla. He has tension in his body, but not too much.

♂ Anchor to your masculine energy – Connect to your masculine energy.

Clench your right fist. Feel every word whilst you read the section below.

If you have one of our *Banish The Bitch* bracelets, wear it on your right wrist. Feel the bracelet acting as an anchor and allow it to store and remind you of the feelings below.

If you need to feel these feelings throughout the day, simply clench your right fist or wear your bracelet on your right wrist to re-establish your anchor.

Take a few deep breaths.

Picture an obstacle or goal in your mind that you wish to conquer. It doesn't matter how small or how big that goal is. Think of something you have been putting off.

Feel what it would be like to have it completed.

You goal might be:

- Getting fit and losing a few pounds.
- Completing a course or study.
- Getting the ironing done and cleaning the house.
- Waking up early to watch a sunrise.
- Starting to grow a vegetable garden.
- Converting three new prospects at work.
- Starting a business.

Picture how you will feel after you achieve your outcome. See your goal or outcome completed.

Chapter 2: Masculine energy

> Take a pen and a piece of paper and create a list of tasks that need to be done to accomplish your outcome. Make sure you tick the tasks off as you go.
>
> Use discipline and focus. We are using our masculine energy.
>
> Anytime you want to feel those feelings, hold your Banish the Bitch bracelet in your right hand or clench your right fist tight and remember the feelings.

Learn to say 'no'

As I discussed last chapter, a big part of being feminine is learning to say 'yes' to gifts, opportunities, compliments and more. To feel feminine, you need to allow yourself to be open to receive.

Masculine energy, on the other hand, often needs to say 'no' to remain focused. If you are at work and you are in your masculine energy and have a vision, goals or an outcome that you're working towards, you need to stay true to it. If you don't agree with something that you feel strongly about, you need to speak up.

This doesn't mean you take total control or relinquish your feminine side – you are just saying 'no' when it's appropriate so you can follow your goals and your passions. It doesn't mean you're rejecting whoever or whatever you're saying 'no' to; it just means you want to stay focused.

How did we become masculine?

We may have flicked the switch to masculine for a number of reasons:

- Our upbringing – We may have needed masculine energy for our survival.
- Our drive for success – We may have wanted to feel significant, powerful, strong and in control.

To alleviate our own anxiety – Waiting for things to happen could have caused us anxiety; we may have decided to take over a situation in order to help us feel more certain.

Leanne and Peter dated for over four years. Peter always liked to organise everything but he always left everything until the last minute. Leanne constantly felt anxious because she never knew what was happening. Everything always felt up in the air. At times, she would decide to take over and organise things so that she could relax again. It made her feel masculine but she also felt better because then she didn't have to worry about it anymore. It gave her certainty.

Leanne tried to communicate to Peter that leaving things to the last minute made her anxious, however, it was just the way Peter was. She was never going to change him. She decided, as hard as it was, if there were no concrete plans made, she would just move ahead and if other things came up for her to do in the meantime, she would organise them. Sometimes he would then try to organise last minute things on the same day. This demonstrated to him that if he wanted her to go with him, he needed to be respectful of her time too and plan in advance.

My lesson

After learning a lot about masculine and feminine energy, I believed that, in order to find the love of my life, I needed to be feminine. I believed it was wrong for me to be masculine at any time.

As a result, I made the decision to surrender my power. I virtually gave up my business, I walked away from my career and I also lost a lot of money.

In my masculine energy, I was stressed and under enormous amounts of pressure, but that was not my problem. The problem was that I was in my masculine energy most of the time. I didn't have balance. I also put myself in the position of *needing* to do what I did at work instead of *choosing* to do it. I made myself the driving force. I trapped myself into a little corner with no way out. There was a way out, of course; I just couldn't see it.

Chapter 2: Masculine energy

After I moved the full spectrum to become totally feminine, I looked back at my past life in masculine energy and thought: Why did I do that? Why did I surrender my power? I loved being in my masculine energy at work. I loved achieving goals. I loved getting deals together. I loved managing staff. I loved the significance of my job. I was extremely happy being in my masculine energy – they were some of the best times of my life.

In my pursuit of becoming feminine, I ran away from all of that. I ran away from the responsibility. I ran because I thought that masculine energy was wrong.

It's not. Like anything, we have to have balance.

~ What masculine men say ~

David from Barcelona said that when he first meets a woman and she's in her masculine energy, it can feel like she's trying to assert her dominance over him, trying to make him feel inferior with her actions.

Summary

If only I knew then what I know now...

You need to know how to access masculine energy when you need to be tough and when you need to stand up for yourself.

- By understanding masculine energy, you will be able to identify a masculine man before you become involved in a relationship. You will also be able to relate to him better and create a better relationship for both of you.

Banish The Bitch And Bring Out The Babe

- Many women resist their masculine energy, not wanting to become intimidating or domineering, or to lose sight of who they are. What they don't realise is that the goal is to be able to access both energies when they need them.

- When you meet a man, don't treat him as competition. Don't immediately blurt out your occupation, your resume and your list of assets. You're not applying for a job; you're getting to know someone. In saying that, you might want to treat moving forward a little like a job application, in that if he's not the right person – do not proceed.

Exercises

1. Now you understand masculine energy, close your eyes and see yourself strong and empowered. Picture what you would look like, what you would sound like and what it would feel like. Feel those feelings of unstoppable strength.

2. In the current version of yourself, do you feel you need to adopt more or less masculine energy in sections of your life than you are currently using? Why? What will happen if you don't?

3. Think of a time when you have used too much masculine energy. Think of a time where it had a negative effect on you. Think of what you could have done differently to manage the situation.

Chapter 3: Integration

I love myself when the feminine blends with the masculine and they begin to balance perfectly.

Once I identified that I was masculine in my energy, I went on a journey to become feminine.

Many women who are masculine in their energy might question this. To powerful, independent women, 'feminine' means weak, helpless and reliant on a man.

When I was in my masculine, I really couldn't see the point of being feminine. I couldn't understand why anyone would want to be feminine, especially when I could do most things myself.

When you're in your masculine energy, you feel unstoppable and you feel strong – why would anyone want to relinquish that feeling? Why would anyone want to go to number two on the food chain?

In my case, I was tired of being strong. I felt exhausted. I wanted to feel love. I wanted to drop the barriers and walls that I had erected. I hadn't let anyone get close to me for so long that I felt numb. The barriers I had erected were like an invisible force field that helped keep people away. I craved love, connection and freedom. I also needed a good cry (probably about ten years' worth).

My stomach was in knots and I had a massive pain in my heart. It was like all the love that I felt had been trapped in my heart. My heart was *aching*. Do you know that feeling?

I knew that I didn't enjoy life like I should and I didn't feel love at the deepest level. While I had material things, I was unhappy. I didn't realise that it was because I was permanently in my masculine energy.

I then went to the opposite end of the scale. I didn't want to be stressed, I didn't want to be disciplined, and I did not want to be a man! I did everything to avoid feeling like a man. Instead of kicking butt in the business world, my purpose became finding love. Once I found love, then it became about the connection with my partner and then my son, and my family and friends.

The pivotal point for me to really embrace and understand my femininity was after I had a baby.

Whether you have children or not, take a moment to imagine having a newborn child and being a stay-at-home mum for a while. When your main role becomes taking care of your baby, it's very easy to feel feminine. Because you're free from work for a while, you're free to be, to nurture and to love. These are very feminine qualities.

If you've been in a high-powered career or a very masculine space for some time, this can be a massive shock to the system. You are out of control. The world you knew has vanished – you're no longer the go-getter or the one who gets shit done! You're now dealing with a whole different kind of shit (yes – literally).

You might feel like you've lost your identity.

The way you've described yourself for so long no longer applies. You're no longer the highly-paid executive, the business owner, the bread-winner or the salesperson. You're now a wife, a partner and a mother.

It's different and it *feels* different.

In my case, after having a baby, I was a mum first and foremost and not a business person anymore. Life wasn't about me anymore; it was about my son. My son became my main focus for many reasons.

Ultimately, I stopped accessing my masculine energy and I became too feminine. I ended up feeling out of sorts. I lost my self-confidence in business. I lost some of my strength. I also lost my drive to succeed.

Looking back, I realised it was because I was focused on what I *didn't* want to go back to. I didn't want to go back to what I felt was the masculine dark side. I thought it was wrong to have any kind of masculine energy.

I was scared that if I introduced any traces of masculine energy, I would take on my masculine persona again, kind of like how a drug addict or alcoholic picks up where they left off. I was scared that I would become my old identity again and that I would not be able to control it.

What I didn't understand was that I could balance my energy. I could flick the switch.

> *The woman's mission is not to enhance the masculine spirit, but to express the feminine; hers is not to preserve a man-made world, but to create a human world by the infusion of the feminine element into all of its activities.*
>
> – Margaret Thatcher

The need for integration

Each energy has its purpose, and it's only through having a healthy balance of the two that you can create a balanced and fulfilling life and relationship.

If you live totally in your feminine energy, it could be hard to achieve some of the things you would like to achieve. Feminine energy is not directed; it's not focused on specific outcomes. It's erratic and it can be easily distracted.

On the other hand, if you live constantly in your masculine energy, you will most likely achieve professionally and you will feel in control of a lot of things. However, you will also feel stressed because you won't be able to control everything that you would like to control. If you're totally focused on living in your masculine energy, it's easy to lose your sense of fun and adventure as you set up the foundations for your professional life.

If you're not quite in either energy, you can feel vulnerable, you can feel lost and you can feel alone. You can feel like a piece of paper that's being blown around in the wind. You can feel sad, lonely, lost and confused.

The key is being able to call on both energies to fill your needs.

Anthony Robbins's model *The Six Human Needs* states that everyone needs to have the following in their lives:

- Love and connection
- Significance
- Certainty
- Variety/uncertainty
- Growth
- Spirituality/contribution

According to Tony, we must have these needs met so we can be happy, though the priority and the intensity of our desire to meet these needs may change depending on what we are focusing on in our life at the time.

Decisions we make are guided by the desire to fill these needs. If our highest need is love, for instance, we may make a decision to skip work and spend the day with our partner. If our highest need is significance, we may make buying a Ferrari a priority, even if we can't really afford it.

If something or someone fills three or more of our needs, we can become addicted to it or them. For example, if you are dating someone and you feel love and connection from that person, if they make you feel significant, they give you variety, and they help you learn and grow, there is a good chance that you are going to feel addicted to them because they fill your needs at a high level. By the same token, if you can fill someone's needs like that, they could become addicted to you (hint, hint).

When it comes to meeting your needs, you can meet them to a certain degree in either a masculine or feminine way.

- **Filling our needs the masculine way –** In our masculine energy, we are motivated by significance and certainty. Work can definitely fill these needs, as succeeding and conquering can make us feel elated and on top of the world. We feel invincible in a powerful way. By using masculine energy, we can be fulfilled by focusing on our vision or goals. Living permanently in our masculine, we could feel tired, overwhelmed and worn out. We probably won't feel totally fulfilled either without the love of an intimate partner.

- **Filling your needs the feminine way –** Feeling love, connection and certainty is the desire of the feminine. Feeling love creates a deep feeling of peace, kind of like when you are really cold and get into a hot bath – love warms you to your core. Love can allow you to feel invincible in a peaceful, calm way. However, by being in your total feminine energy, you may miss opportunities to tap into your masculine energy to achieve massive goals, particularly at work or in business.

Our aim is to learn how to fill our needs in both energies. So we can feel and experience our power, and feel and experience love. This is what integration is all about. This is where a lot of people experience fulfilment.

The 5 levels of masculine to feminine energy for women.

Where do you sit right now? What level are you at? Take a good, honest look.

Banish The Bitch And Bring Out The Babe

1. **Masculine** – She's very masculine in her behaviour. Men can find her intimidating. She likes to be right and she likes to try to control the situation. At times, she can seem competitive and even aggressive in her behaviour.

2. **Integrated woman** – She has access to both energies. She has access to masculine energy when she needs to get things done or when she needs to defend herself. She also has access to feminine energy when she wants to experience love. She can 'be', 'do' and 'love'. She's centred and in control.

3. **Feminine energy** – She is feminine in every sense of the word. She looks, speaks and acts feminine. She's centred and happy. She radiates love. She is focused on being, not doing. She enjoys connecting to nature and connecting to people.

4. **Soft feminine** – She has low self-confidence and low self-esteem. Most things she does, to the outside world, look like a cry for help. She may even look like she's waiting for someone to save her.

5. **Submissive feminine** – She operates out of fear. She very rarely has a voice of her own. She generally agrees with everyone and she may be involved with a domineering man. She is loving and caring. She may feel she needs to be with a man to help her feel stable.

Which energy are you living in now?

Is it predominantly masculine or feminine?

Reflect on the different traits described in the last two chapters and ask yourself:

- How do you feel when you are alone? Do you feel more masculine or more feminine in your own company? Do you even feel neutral?
- How do you feel when you are with your family?

Chapter 3: Integration

- How do you feel when you meet new people?
- How do you feel when you are being creative or when you are in your flow?
- How do you feel when you are at work?
- If you are in a relationship, how do you feel in your relationship? How do you feel when you are with your partner?
- If you are in a relationship, what energy do you perceive your partner to be in?

If you're having trouble figuring out which energy you're in, consider the following and how you feel when you are in these emotions.

When you are in your masculine energy, you are more than likely operating out of power emotions.

- When you're in your masculine energy, you will experience powerful emotions such as determination, strength, discipline, focus and success.
- If you have too much masculine energy, you could be perceived to be pushy, argumentative, selfish, angry and stubborn.

When you are in your feminine energy, you are operating more out of fear emotions.

- When you're in your feminine energy, you are in your heart. You feel love. You love helping and taking care of people.
- If you have too much feminine energy, you may crave more certainty and more love. If you don't manage it properly, fear or uncertainty can make you feel like you're going crazy. You can feel all over the place. You can literally feel unbalanced.

When you display the masculine energy traits and emotions, you are in your masculine energy, and when you display the feminine energy traits and emotions, you are in your feminine energy.

As I've already discussed, it's important to have a balance of both energies, but one will usually feel like the energy you *need* to use for certain situations or activities, and the other will feel like the one you *want* to live in more of the time.

In your case, where do you feel comfortable? Ideally, you will spend the majority of your time in this energy, and flick the switch to the other one as needed.

Remember that there is no wrong or right way to feel – it's about how you *want* to feel.

If you are still having trouble working out what energy you may be in, you can do what I did – ask people. Don't be upset at their answer, though; maybe it's what you need to hear. Ask them what you did for them to believe that about you.

How to integrate both energies

An integrated woman has access to both energies. She has access to masculine energy when she needs to get things done or when she needs to defend herself. She also has access to feminine energy when she wants to experience love. She's centred and in control.

If you're totally feminine, you need to incorporate some masculine traits for survival and for your protection. If you're totally masculine, you need to incorporate some feminine traits for relaxation and fun to ensure you stay in balance. The key is being able to adopt each energy as needed to maintain your happiness and balance.

If you can access both energies, if you need to look after yourself and protect yourself or your family, you can. If you want to relax, unwind and experience fun and relaxation and pleasure, you also can. By experiencing both, you will understand the difference in feelings

Chapter 3: Integration

between feminine and masculine energy, and you will also be able to see it in others a mile away.

When you focus on your masculine energy, you will become emotionally stronger and tougher, more directed and more focused. You will have your eye on your outcomes. You will eliminate distractions and you will live a much more disciplined life. Your confidence will grow as you build faith in yourself.

How can you do it? In the rest of this chapter I'll discuss bringing your masculine and feminine energies into different parts of your life.

However, note that once you start your integration of the two energies, you may experience some uncomfortable feelings. When I first made the transition from masculine to feminine energy, I found the confrontational energy of a masculine woman difficult. I could see the old me in her and I didn't like it. She also made me feel like I needed to compete with her. I must admit that I still have those same uncomfortable feelings sometimes, but I recognise this and I choose not to compete with her. I really have no interest in doing so.

After recognising the energy in some of your friends, you may find that you change your friends or how much time you spend with them. You could prefer to hang around girlfriends with the same energy as you. Or you could just accept all of them, as you now understand where they are coming from.

How to make decisions with both energies

The most successful people in the world don't make big decisions on their own. CEOs have a board of directors, athletes have a suite of coaches and trainers, academics have supervisors, and even artists have mentors and teachers. So why do we try to go it alone?

I want you to realise that you are not alone – you have your own board of directors, a team of people that live right inside of you.

These people are The Fighter, The Lover, The Comedian and The Queen.

Banish The Bitch And Bring Out The Babe

We all have different emotions in our body, and different personality types that show up in different situations. We have four characters, each of which represents a different type of energy or emotion.

- The Fighter is your masculine energy – this part of you is directed, focused and strong.
- The Lover is your feminine energy – she is loving, nurturing, free-flowing and intuitive.
- The Comedian is the playful part of you – you could imagine The Comedian as a joyful, playful inner child.
- The Queen is your higher self – she is the governing body who makes the final decision after calling on the wisdom of the other three on your team. Her purpose is to serve the greater good.

When you are about to make a decision, consider what each of these personality types would do in the situation. Bring all four perspectives to the table. They will help you to gain clarity and integrate your energies. They will ensure you are not stuck in one frame of mind or one emotion.

They will also have different views on the consequences or benefits of any decision, which you can weigh up to make sure you do what's right for you. Ask The Lover, ask The Fighter, ask The Comedian and then ask The Queen. Once The Queen has weighed up these consequences and benefits, if she is comfortable, go ahead. If not, don't.

Always follow your heart, but take your brain with you.

A different way to set goals

As a woman who was an achiever, a goal setter and someone who was seen as successful, I operated from masculine energy in the workplace and in life. At the time, I thrived on it. It made me feel important, it made me feel significant and it made me feel special.

I remember doing a personality profiling test at the time that asked if I would stop to smell the roses if I was walking through a park. I seriously remember thinking, 'Why the heck would anyone do that? What a waste of time!'

Goal setting is traditionally very masculine – think of long 'to do' lists and measurable outcomes. While masculine energy is very driven to achieve these goals, if your core energy is feminine, it can be very stressful, especially if you don't reach those goals.

So is it possible to approach goal setting from a feminine perspective? Absolutely.

You can simply visualise how you want to *feel*. Masculine energy is about 'doing' while feminine energy is about 'being'. For example, the masculine might say, 'I want to make $50,000 in the next three months.' The feminine might say, 'I want to feel certain, financially secure and happy.' While both might want the same monetary value, the feminine is also focused on the feelings.

♀ Anchor to your feminine energy – Connect to your feminine energy.

Clench your left fist. Feel every word whilst you read the section below

What feelings do you wish to feel in the next week?

Do you want to feel successful, confident, happy, sexy, secure, loved, cherished, healthy, proud, grateful, something else or all of the above?

Choose some feelings you want to experience and write them down. Visualise feeling that way. Give yourself an opportunity to really *feel* the emotion – what it will feel like to achieve that feeling.

Banish The Bitch And Bring Out The Babe

> ♂ **Anchor to your masculine energy – Connect to your masculine energy.**
>
> Now clench your right fist. Feel every word whilst you read the section below.
>
> Connect to your masculine energy. Ask yourself exactly what has to happen and what you need to do for you to feel the emotions you have listed. Can anyone else help you? What else can you do?
>
> Write down the feelings you wish to feel, then a list of everything you need to do to feel those feelings. You can categorise them into different areas if you like.
>
> I have asked you to do this exercise in both your feminine and masculine energy as you needed to feel the feelings and also focus on writing your list. Your feminine energy will focus on the feeling, and your masculine energy will focus on the 'to do' list.

Dealing with overwhelm

Jodi struggled when it came to her taxation commitments. She saw the whole process as painful. The paperwork covered her desk along with the bills she needed to pay. She took one look at it all and it made her incredibly anxious. It didn't help that she had a belief that she was no good with figures and taxation.

She knew it would take her a while to process everything. It scared her – all of the paperwork sitting on her desk combined with the bills she had to pay. It represented money she knew was going to walk out the door. Money she knew that she needed.

When you are in your feminine energy, overwhelm can be paralysing. The feminine can easily suffer anxiety or feel uneasy at the thought of completing a long list of tasks when she has so many things that need to be finished.

When you are in overwhelm, it's time to get into your masculine energy. You need to prioritise what's most important and then focus on one task or category at a time. Do your best to finish it. In most cases, you'll discover that the tasks themselves aren't as difficult as you expected, and once you start making progress, it won't take that long to get through them after all.

In Jodi's case, she just needed to make a start. Once she began, she needed to hit that sucker on the head. Once she finished one thing and got a quick win, that would power her to move on to the next thing.

Once you make a start, you can complete something and take something off your 'to do' list. You will feel a sense of relief and a sense of completion.

Feminine leadership

Like goals, leadership is another area that is seen as being masculine. In my businesses, at the start I lead like a man. I thought I had to. However, the following experience changed my leadership style forever.

I watched a dramatic and graphic video some years back demonstrating very different leadership styles relating to teams competing in an *Eco-Challenge*. Each team comprised a regulated mix of both men and women. They raced for twenty-four hours a day over a rugged 500-kilometre course that involved trekking, canoeing and mountain biking. From memory, they had to complete the course in twelve days.

The video showed the difference between the leaders and their motivations for wanting to win.

The first leader was a female who had previously participated in an *Eco-Challenge*. The previous year, she was close to winning, however, something happened to her bike and she had to pull out of the competition. She re-entered the competition the following year with the goal to win.

When the filmmakers spoke to her team, what was interesting was that the team wanted to win for her. When they interviewed her, she also wanted the team to win for her. Ultimately, her outcome was only about her. It appeared she didn't care about her team at all. They soon lost interest in her vision.

The next team was from New Zealand. They had the bright idea that they would not eat or sleep – they would just run. The idea was to get a jump-start on everyone else. In the end, they ended up fatigued and de-hydrated and nearly all got carried off on stretchers.

In the third team, I would describe the leader as integrated. He wanted to win and he also really cared about his team. When someone was hurting, he organised help for them. He made sure his team felt supported and protected. He nurtured, supported and looked after them. It wasn't about him; it was about his team doing it together. He lead from the front but also followed up from behind.

Guess which team won? The third team.

This is a great demonstration that proves that if you are in business, it will help to be integrated in both energies in the workplace.

Masculine leaders tend to focus on the outcome. They know there will be casualties along the way and they factor those in. They are decisive and they want to win. They plan, they try to calculate risks and they prepare for battle. When tough decisions need to be made, they make them.

Feminine leaders, on the other hand, do not lead like alpha males. They become like a lioness with her cubs – strict, caring, fun, balanced, nurturing and fiercely protective. They allow those on their team to make decisions, take responsibility and grow. They lead from the front by offering direction and support. When they come from an authentic place, people will do more for them; they know they care about them as much as the goal.

When you are integrated in your energies, you can draw on each of these qualities.

Bringing femininity into the business world

Most business tasks use masculine energy – negotiating deals, meeting deadlines, solving problems and more. So where does feminine energy fit in if you want to be an integrated woman?

If you are *too feminine* in business, you could end up keeping non-performing staff, effectively paying them to be your friends rather than making the hard decisions to performance-manage or terminate them. You are likely to allow too many distractions and may lose sight of the big picture.

Some women struggle to reconcile their masculine and feminine energies in business. Bridgette, for instance, was a single mother with two children. Her highest values were love and connection, and she became focused on seeking the attention of others to make her happy. As a result, she waited for the phone to ring, she'd call friends and family, she engaged on social media and she frequently checked emails. She would look wherever she could to get a hint of connection (a very feminine trait).

Ultimately, though, Bridgette struggled to earn an income. When she had love and connection first, she never got anything done. She was too busy trying to get external attention rather than focusing on her goals. To be effective, she realised she had to make love and connection her number two priority. She had to rearrange her priorities and put success first. For her, that was the right thing to do.

If you are permanently in love and connection mode, when you need to achieve results, you'll struggle to get much done, especially if you are working for yourself from home. Because of this, you may need to adopt some masculine energy, or employ a masculine coach or an accountability partner who will kick your butt if you go off track.

At the other end of the spectrum are the women who aim to be masculine at work, and, therefore, overcompensate for being a woman. They feel like they need to try and be even more masculine and aggressive. These women sometimes lose sight of the outcome and make it more about the argument, which lessens their effectiveness.

Finally, there is the masculine woman in the workplace who tries to put on a feminine persona to manipulate. You know the kind of girl – the one who turns up to a business meeting with a short skirt and her boobs hanging out. Inexperienced or younger men may not always get it. More experienced and aware men, and nearly all women, will see straight through it.

In the boardroom, when a masculine woman shows her cleavage and she wears a short shirt, it's like a man flirting with another man. It's also an insult to any man who knows what she's up to. It can be obvious to him that she knows she's not going to get by on her intellect alone and that she's trying to use her 'assets' to get what she wants.

If you want to be taken seriously around a boardroom table, the only assets you need on display are your brains and personality. Please put your other 'assets' away.

If you are *too masculine* in your business, you will be stressed and you will be tired. At times, you will feel incredible pressure. You may also have good staff leave you for being too busy focusing on the goal and not your team.

On the other hand, being integrated in the workplace allows you to have access to feminine energy. You will love and support your staff and make sure, to a degree, that they are okay and that they have everything they need to succeed. Meanwhile, your masculine energy will keep you accountable; it will also make sure things happen when they need to. Your masculine energy will keep you in check and keep your staff in check. In business, we still need to focus on the bottom line – how to make sales and how to make money. After all, that's why we're in business. The masculine focuses on the business succeeding.

When you put the energies together, a feminine woman using masculine energy tends to use her energy to focus on how to benefit her clients while making money and, therefore, benefitting the business. She creates win-win situations for all.

So how can you be integrated with feminine and masculine energies in the workplace?

Chapter 3: Integration

Your rules of engagement

You need to have rules for your energy at work and at home. I call them your rules of engagement.

When you are at work, realise that you might have to be in your masculine. You might have to fight battles and you might have to win.

However, you don't need to fight and win all the time. When you go out with a man or you are with a group of men and they say things you don't agree with, weigh up if it really matters enough to argue with them. You can try to impress them with your intelligence or you might even like to try to win the argument, but realise this – it's unlikely that you will win the men over. If you are confrontational with men, they will see you as aggressive and masculine and they will treat you like a man. You need to decide what's more important to you.

When you are at home, on the other hand, you can be feminine with your friends or with family. You have your feminine rules of engagement. When you are with your friends, don't look to fight and win battles. After all, what's more important – having friends or winning? If you want friends, practise the art of biting your tongue!

Relax. Be in the moment. Make sure your barriers are down and be open to getting to know people better than you ever have before.

When you are around people, make sure you are aware of your energy and flick your switch accordingly.

> *Debate is masculine, conversation is feminine.*
>
> – Amos Bronson Alcott

Banish The Bitch And Bring Out The Babe

♀ Anchor to your feminine energy – Connect to your feminine energy.

Clench your left fist. Feel every word whilst you read the section below.

If you have one of our *Banish The Bitch* bracelets, wear it on your left wrist. Feel the bracelet acting as an anchor and allow it to store and remind you of the feelings below.

If you need to feel these feelings throughout the day, simply clench your left fist or wear your bracelet on your left wrist to re-establish your anchor.

How do you adapt from being masculine at work to feminine at home?

Once you shut the door and turn the key at work, take on another persona. Be the fun and flirty, happy girl you are. Some women like to make up names for themselves. If your name is Chris at work, when you leave work, be Chrissy instead. If you are known as Sam at work, be Sammy at home. You can take on another persona in your mind. You don't have to physically change anything or tell anyone. Make it fun for you.

Shake off the day. When you leave work, sing along to music on the way home in the car or talk to some feminine girlfriends on the phone. When you get home, take your work clothes off, if you can, have a bath and put on some nice, feminine clothes.

Make sure you flick your *Banish the Bitch* bracelet to feminine when you get home, thereby flicking the switch to shift your energy.

Connecting with other women

Do you find that you just can't seem to relate to other women in general? Do you have a lot of female friendships that seem to fall by the wayside? Do you have trouble bonding or have trouble forming *deep* connections with other women? Does it feel like they are all surface relationships?

Some women are so far into their masculine energy that they don't see what's happening. They have no clue. They often complain that other women are bitches and complain about what they do and don't do. If you've been in this position, it might be time to check in with *your* energy. While you might not like to admit it, you may very well be swimming in your masculine energy.

A lot of masculine women wonder why they don't have a lot of strong female relationships. They may even prefer the company of men.

This is why.

Masculine women can have issues with other masculine women because they see them as competition. They may think that the other women could demonstrate that they are smarter, more successful or more qualified than they are. This makes them feel threatened.

While they are in their masculine energy, though, they can still have feminine emotions attached. Sometimes they find it hard to juggle the two emotions. They want to win (masculine energy), but they also really want to be liked and accepted (feminine energy).

So what can you do?

Please listen to what I am about to say. This is the key to *everything*.

This alone will affect so many things in your life. It will affect your friendships, relationships, children and could ultimately affect your happiness.

If you are masculine in your energy, I will say this in a direct way, in a way that you need to hear it. Hold onto your testicles, ladies.

Banish The Bitch And Bring Out The Babe

These are my tips:

- Please don't talk down to people as if you're smarter than they are. Also don't talk over them.

- Accept that not everyone will have the same opinion as you, and it will help if you bite your tongue a lot more often. I'm not saying not to express yourself, not to have a voice, or not to stand up for yourself, but to pick your battles. Does having an argument with someone really matter? Will trying to change their opinion really make a difference to your life?

- Don't try to control everyone and everything – it upsets you and it stresses you out. Instead, acknowledge that it's impossible to control everyone. Not everyone will do what you want them to do when you want them to do it.

- You might not like it when others control a situation or when someone else organises something. Calm down – it's okay. Yes, you have your own ideas on how you would like to have things run and you could organise it far better. But just enjoy the fact that someone else is doing it. In the scheme of life, it's no big deal.

- You don't need to know everything about every topic. Give others the opportunity to shine.

- Relax and start to build friendships. Try and be liked for who you are, not what you can do. Take a breath. Start to enjoy every moment.

If you don't balance your energy, you will find it hard to be another woman's 'best girlfriend'. You will never find someone with whom you could have a lifelong connection, with whom you could share your deepest secrets, who understands you and who loves you. Until you drop the barriers, you will only ever be their competition.

Summary

If only I knew then what I know now...

- It's only through having a healthy balance of masculine and feminine energy that you can create a fulfilling life and deep relationships. If you live totally in your feminine energy, it could be hard to achieve some of the things you would like to achieve, while if you live constantly in your masculine energy, you will feel stressed because you can't control everything that you would like to control and you could lose your sense of fun and adventure.
- According to Tony Robbins, our six human needs are love and connection, significance, certainty, variety/uncertainty, growth and spirituality/contribution. I believe that we can meet these needs in a masculine way, in a feminine way, or by using both energies.
- You can use your feminine energy when making decisions, setting goals, leading others and connecting with others when you want to build relationships and experience your emotions. You can use your masculine energy when you need to defend yourself or get things done.

Exercises

1. Think about six women you know. Based on what you have learnt so far, identify who has predominantly masculine and who has predominantly feminine energy.
2. Think about six men you know. Who is masculine and who is feminine in their energy?

Banish The Bitch And Bring Out The Babe

3. Now think about your relationships with those people. Who do you relate to more? Who would you like to emulate in your energy?

Part 2

Finding Mr Right

Chapter 4: Polarity and attraction

You ask me why I like you? To be honest, I really don't know why I like you. There is just something about you that I love. Your smile, and how you make me feel. How you make me laugh. Something about you draws me to you and I can't get you out of my head.

We have all heard the saying that opposites attract. We know this is true – take a magnet, for example. If we were to get two magnets and we put the north and south poles together, they will attract each other. Yet if you put two north poles or two south poles together, they will repel. It's the same principle when it comes to masculine and feminine energy in relationships.

Pole (opposite): *Either of two completely opposite or different opinions, positions or qualities.*

Polar: *Polar opposites are complete opposites.*

Polarity: *The quality of being opposite.*

Does it mean that if you are a truck driver then your perfect partner is a florist? Does it mean if you are a fitness coach your perfect match is a couch potato?

Not necessarily.

Masculine energy searches for feminine energy. When they are together in a relationship, each feels complete, as each one balances the other. The masculine feels balanced, in that he can relax and take his mind off the things that are potentially worrying him. Meanwhile, the feminine feels calm, safe and protected. When a feminine woman is around a masculine man, it makes her feel more feminine because she doesn't have to worry about taking care of everything.

However, this is only possible when there's a balance between the two energies.

When a woman is feminine with a masculine man, it feels similar to her being a little girl again. He loves that he can take care of her. He can be her protector, her lover and at the same time, he feels needed and that makes him happy. She feels looked after, she feels protected and she can be herself. She can relax and laugh; she doesn't need to worry. They can have fun together. She also helps him to not take life so seriously.

When a woman is strong and successful and spends a lot of time in her masculine energy, she might notice that some men do not have as much masculine energy as her. As I discussed earlier, this can lead some men to feel intimidated, while others will just be repelled like the two north or south poles of a magnet. For a man to handle a woman like this, he needs to be extra strong and have a clear vision, otherwise polarity in the relationship will be challenged. This will help her feel feminine in the relationship. Otherwise, she might consider a more feminine man to create polarity.

Similarly, if a man's masculine energy is weak, he won't be confident. His goals or outcomes will be weak and he'll worry about failure. If he doesn't step up, the woman in the relationship may take over the masculine role. The danger is that she may realise that she can do

Chapter 4: Polarity and attraction

everything for herself, including earn the income, take care of the kids, run the house and everything else that needs doing. He may just make himself obsolete – he won't feel needed. This is where relationships start to deteriorate from the woman's perspective. She could begin to think that she doesn't really need a man. She may also be quite happy controlling things… for now. She begins by picking up the dropped ball, then the next minute she's propelled further into that lifestyle. In a few months or years, she becomes tired and worn out. She reaches the stage where she's sick of being so darn strong all the time. She ends up totally unhappy and unfulfilled and realises too late that she has no polarity with her current partner.

If this happens, especially if masculine energy isn't the woman's preferred state, the woman may not only resent him, but will lose respect for him if she feels he's not taking care of her and protecting her. She'll think, 'Why do I need a man if I'm doing everything myself?'

Most feminine women want a man they can rely on. They want a man who's more masculine than they are. They want him to step up, to take the lead and to take care of them. They want a man who's directed, centred and calm – a man who allows them to be their own person. They yearn for someone who wants to take care of them and protect them, especially when they have small children. They want someone who has their back, as they will have his.

If a man is very feminine, like the masculine woman, he needs either to find a woman who is much more feminine than he is to help boost his masculine energy or to embrace his feminine side to have polarity in the relationship. He may need to attract a woman who's masculine at her core.

In any case, the people in a relationship need to represent opposite energies to complement each other's strengths and weaknesses.

The expected makes a relationship certain and the unexpected makes it passionate.

Do you attract men who have feminine energy?

Chances are, if feminine men are attracted to you, they could see you as someone who could complement or supplement them where they are weak. For example, if you are strong, they may subconsciously feel attracted to your strength. If they are looking for balance in their life, you could be the one that they think will help them achieve that balance. You could have what they feel they are lacking.

You could also be attracted to a feminine man for varying reasons. A common one is when a man appears to be 'safe'. If you have a strong need for control, you may feel reassurance that you can control him to some extent. It might make him more attractive to you. You may feel safe as you think that it's unlikely that he'll ever leave you. He could fill your need for stability. He may, however, not fill your needs in other ways.

Someone you feel 'safe' with may not give you the passion you desire.

~ What masculine men say ~

Lenny from Sydney said, instead of just asking how women can be more feminine, the question should also be, 'Why aren't men more masculine?' If men showed up this way, then women would feel safe to be feminine.

Why is polarity important?

Understanding and creating polarity is important for a number of reasons:

- Understanding polarity gives you the power to attract the men you want. If you are attracted to masculine men who have a clear vision and direction, who are centred, strong, emotionally stable and who are trustworthy, they will be attracted to feminine women who are free, happy, radiant and fun.

Chapter 4: Polarity and attraction

- Polarity is nature's aphrodisiac. If you are totally feminine and your man is totally masculine, you will have polarity, which results in attraction or chemistry.

- If you find someone you have an amazing connection with – through your communication and through your intimate relationship – maintaining polarity will help to keep the relationship long-lasting. After all, if you can feel each other's deepest feelings and blow each other's minds making love, then there would be no reason to want to end the relationship!

Creating polarity

To create polarity in a relationship, or to find a man with whom you will have polarity, you need to be clear on two things – the role you want to have in the relationship, and the role you want your man to have.

Define your role in the relationship

How do you want the polarity to be in your relationship?

Although we all need to use masculine and feminine energy in different situations, in your ideal relationship you will have one primary role – either the feminine or the masculine. By knowing which role you'd prefer up front, you can find a man who complements that role.

Ultimately, there is nothing more attractive to a masculine man than a truly feminine woman and vice versa. So if you are currently quite masculine in your energy and you would like to be feminine, you need to find a man who's more masculine in his energy than you. When you find him, you will feel feminine. You won't have to try. He will want to take care of you. (And he won't take your crap, either.)

Banish The Bitch And Bring Out The Babe

I think of masculine and feminine energy like two sides to a battery. There's a plus side and a minus side, and in order to make something turn on, you need to have opposites touching. It's the same in relationships.

– Tracy McMillan

Feminine women – Personality types

If you would like to be the feminine energy in your relationship, then that's about letting go of trying to control everything. This will allow a man to step in and take the leading role.

However, keep in mind that not all feminine personality types are healthy. Here are some different feminine personalities:

- **Feminine –** She's feminine in every sense of the word. She radiates love. She's happy and she is centred. She cares about and loves others (sometimes to her own detriment). She doesn't see her partner as competition. She allows her man to take control, she trusts and she has faith. She's happy to surrender some parts of herself to her man.

- **Lover –** She does everything to help the family operate as a family unit. She's loving and she's great at nurturing her children. She loves her friends. Her goal is to keep everyone together, happy and in a loving place. Her love is the glue binding the family together.

- **Helper –** She'll help others whenever they need her. Her friends know they can call on her at any hour of the day or night. She'll help others often to her own detriment by putting her friends' needs above her own. If they abuse the privilege, then there will come a time when she will be less free to give her time and energy.

- **Worrier –** She worries about everything. She will even worry if she has nothing to worry about!

- **Drama queen –** Everything is a drama... even the good things. She will tell everyone all of her problems, thereby connecting with others and herself. She'll probably even post her problems all over social media.
- **Victim –** Everything happens to her and she blames others for everything. It's everyone else's fault.
- **Submissive –** She is scared to speak out and ask for what she wants. She has low self-esteem and, therefore, agrees with everyone. Potentially, she may only be submissive with her partner because she is scared to stand up for herself. He may control her in every way. What she says, what she wears and what she does. She may want to stand up to him, but she never does. Her partner could be the cause, not allowing her to have her own voice.

You may find you fluctuate between different personality types. That's okay. It only begins to be a problem if you live in a destructive personality type all the time.

Masculine women – Personality types

Perhaps you like being in control and calling the shots, and you want that position in your relationship as well as in other parts of your life (like your career). If so, you'll be taking on the role of masculine energy in a relationship.

As with feminine personality types, though, not all masculine personality types are healthy. Here are some different types of masculine personalities:

- **Hard worker –** She works hard and she is very goal-oriented. She has her goals, her outcomes and she knows her purpose. She knows what she wants and she will stop at nothing to achieve it. She looks after her family and she generally doesn't take care of herself as well as she should. She doesn't complain; she just gets on with life. She is the main bread-winner in the family.

- **Controller –** She likes to be in control. People, places and things. She prefers to be the organiser of any events as, when anyone else does it, it's not as good as it could have been under her direction. She believes that everyone should do what she says. She has strict rules and she wants everyone to live by her rules. She also likes to control the man she's with. She can probably even read maps.
- **Bitch –** She hates everyone. She loves to talk and gossip about people behind their backs. She is catty and spiteful. She is jealous of everyone and everything. She hates the world – especially that bitch over there.
- **Manipulator –** She will try to get her own way by manipulation. She has goals and outcomes, she knows what she wants and she aims to get it. Her eye is on the prize. Her boobs and backside could be hanging out on occasion, especially at work.
- **Selfish –** She doesn't think about anyone except herself. It's always about *her*. You may like to look up narcissistic tendencies in a woman.
- **Attention seeker –** She will do anything for attention. See will post anything to social media – including loads of selfies. See will post herself in bikinis just to try to lure men in. She doesn't realise they are probably all talking about her behind her back. She will go out of her way to be seen when she is out. She thinks she has to be loud and obnoxious to attract a man.

Who do you want to be? Analyse honestly who you are being in your relationships. Consider who you are showing up as predominantly, as this will also determine how you are in your relationships. This will determine who you will attract into your life and the level of polarity you will have.

Sometimes we are a combination of the different personality types.

Who are you?

Who do you want as your man?

Who you want as your man should complement the role you want to have in your relationship.

Types of masculine men

If you want to be in your feminine energy, you will need a strong man who can allow you to feel feminine. Most likely, he:

- Is directed and knows what he wants in life.
- Cares about you and he makes decisions based on what's best for you and your family.
- Makes plans for the future and includes you in those plans.
- Knows what he wants and goes about getting it.
- Wants to provide for and protect you and your family.
- Appreciates the joy and adventure you bring to his life, which he can easily miss when focused on his goal.
- Wants to feel supported in his ambitions.

When your man is in his masculine energy and you know he has his vision and his goals and he's going about achieving them, this allows the feminine to feel safe, comfortable and happy. She can trust him to follow through on his word. This then makes your man feel happy and successful.

Keep in mind that we all have a mix of masculine and feminine energy, and the same goes for your man. This doesn't necessarily mean that he's predominantly in his feminine energy – it just means he is connected to it.

Banish The Bitch And Bring Out The Babe

For example, feminine energy in an alpha male could be as subtle as him connecting with his senses and connecting with nature. He will experience feminine energy when he's spending time in his heart rather than his head, such as when he's being loving and nurturing towards his children or when he's having loads of fun playing with them.

When it comes to masculine men, here are some of the different personality types to look out for:

- **Hard worker –** He does his best to provide for you. He's mature. He has a vision for the future. He has an aura of stability. He knows where everyone fits into his picture. He takes care of everyone to the best of his ability and he likes it that way. He loves to take care of his woman and a big motivation is to make her happy. He's a control freak, but in a good way.

- **Team player –** He'll help people, often to the detriment of himself. He'll be the first one to offer to help you move house, or help you fix something. If he feels that someone is taking advantage of him, or he feels like he's being used or taken for granted, he will abruptly stop helping. He doesn't give to get, but he won't tolerate being used. If someone takes advantage of him, he would rather nail his genitals to a burning building than help them again.

- **Pleaser –** He is masculine in his core, however, he's allowed the woman he's with to take control. He's adapted his behaviour to try to protect the relationship. He figures it's easier to be quiet and to keep the peace. He'll do anything to keep his woman happy. He's caring, loving and giving. In order to keep the peace, he doesn't make decisions regarding most aspects of his personal life. He becomes uncertain and weak, therefore, he becomes emasculated. He may overcompensate with more masculine behaviour towards others outside the relationship.

- **User –** He has no morals and no conscience. He's out for what he can get. To him, sex is not the answer. Sex is the question. 'Yes' is the answer.

- **Player –** He plays the game but in a few different courts. He doesn't want to let go of female relationships. He's not happy only having one woman – he likes to hedge his bets. He may be with his wife and a mistress. He has an intense fear of being alone.

- **Loser –** He hangs around beer gardens playing on poker machines all day. He could be a smoker and a heavy drinker and avoids all responsibility. He'll never grow up (thirty-year-old skateboarders would also fit into this category – most of these guys don't have children as the skateboard is their contraceptive).

- **Commitment-phobe –** He's scared of settling down. He says he will do something in the future, however, the future never comes.

- **Wanker –** He knows everything. He's an authority on everything but has never done anything. He generally hangs around other wankers.

- **Dominator or conqueror –** He's extremely selfish and only cares about himself. He throws tantrums if he doesn't get his own way. He expects the world to revolve around him. Do not mistake this as pure masculine. They actually think they are sooooo masculine. He is not; he's an asshole. If this sounds familiar, research narcissistic traits.

If you wish to be feminine in your relationship, aim for the hard worker. He's a real man. He will allow and encourage you to be you. He'll have your back. He'll take care of you. He'll be your rock and your safety net and you will be his.

> *A real man won't try and make you jealous with other women;*
> *he will make other women jealous of how he treats you.*

Types of feminine men

If you want to be in control or wear the pants in the relationship, this is masculine energy. Some women who are masculine in their energy could be happier with the certainty that a more feminine man gives them.

The dynamics of the relationship:

- He will take a back seat, leaving you to be the driving force in the relationship.
- You will most likely be the main bread-winner in the relationship.
- You will feel safe with him – he probably won't ever leave you.
- He will be very loyal.
- He'll always ask for direction and guidance.
- You might feel like you're training him or at times could also feel like you are his mother.
- He is happy to help you achieve your goals.
- He's happy for you to take the lead and he wants you to make the decisions.
- He's not career-focused.

Some women are very happy like this. However, it's important to really think about whether you want to have control all the time. Do you want to be the leader of the family, to make the decisions and to set the direction? Is this your long-term plan?

Feminine men – Personality types

- **Lover –** He loves everyone. He is nurturing and loves his children and his family. He takes his burden of care seriously. He is centred, supportive and at peace with who

Chapter 4: Polarity and attraction

he is. He might not have ambitions at work, but he does for his family. He's so accommodating he even leaves the toilet seat down without being asked.

- **Listener** – He doesn't have many friends; you are his whole world. He is understanding and he listens when you talk. He shows empathy for how you feel. He has all the time in the world for you.

- **Dreamer** – He lives blissfully unaware of real life. He gets distracted very easily, preferring to live in his own little fantasy world. He starts lots of projects but very rarely finishes them.

- **Flapper** – He is always flapping around, never knowing what to do first. He finds it hard to achieve anything because he can't get past the first task. If he has two things on his 'to do' list, to him it feels like two hundred. He's not afraid to express his anxiety to anyone that will listen.

- **She-man** – He is happy for and expects the woman he's with to look after him in every way – emotionally and financially. He never makes decisions. That's your job.

- **Mummy's boy** – He's forty-five years old and still lives with his mum. He's used to having everything done for him – his mum still washes and irons his sheets, his handkerchiefs and his underwear.

- **Victim** – He thinks everything always happens to him and everything is everyone else's fault. He believes everyone else's decisions have caused him to be where he is. He never takes responsibly and will never be accountable for anything.

- **Drama queen** – Everything revolves around him. He tries to be a dominator but, because he constantly complains, no one listens to him anyway.

- **Princess** – Princesses are feminine to the extreme. He is a *diva*. He makes demands as everything is always about him. He's very worried about what people think of him; like a heavily-made-up diva, he hides behind many masks and he bitches about *everyone.*

- **Gym junkie –** If you have a great body but you don't look after your wife and children, your work suffers and you aren't nice to anyone, you're no better than anyone else. You're just a jerk who goes to the gym. Some guys love taking photos of themselves. Some of them are totally in love… with themselves. Nothing else matters in their life except the way they look. Their ego is massive! I'm sure I was in a relationship with someone who got sexually aroused by his own gym photos.

- **Attention seeker –** These guys will do *anything* for attention.

What type of man do you want?

Of course, both masculine and feminine men have their downsides.

The downside of being with a masculine man is that it can seem as though he always prioritises his time at work ahead of you and your family. If he feels he can achieve significance and create long-term certainty for his future in his work, he may focus on it for a large percentage of his time. He will constantly be battling the beast, aiming to conquer and defeat, sometimes at the cost of spending time with you. That's the trade-off for him executing his plans, his vision and for him achieving his success.

Additionally, masculine men can sometimes fight their more feminine feelings, choosing to suppress their emotions. Sometimes they can forget what it's like to feel as feminine energy does and can find it hard to relate to the feminine emotions. It's for this reason that he will avoid dealing with yours.

The downside of being with a feminine man is that you rarely have the opportunity to switch off, let go and be taken care of. Yes, you can ask him to help out or take care of you when you need him to, but you'll probably always be the one initiating and directing this.

In the end, every relationship needs balance. The feminine energy keeps the balance by being carefree, happy and flowing. The masculine energy has strength, direction and leadership. The role you choose is up to you. Your choice will determine whom you attract.

Maintaining polarity

Polarity is a balancing act and, because we can all shift between masculine and feminine energies, it can change in an instant.

Imagine being out with your man and he shrieks when a butterfly flies past him. He yells out that he's petrified of butterflies. How would his masculinity rate, performing like that in front of you? How would the polarity be in the relationship? You would probably wonder what would have happened if there had been a spider or a snake... he would have run a mile! In the worst-case scenario, you may think that he will always run at the first glimpse of trouble and will never hang around to protect you.

To put the shoe on the other foot, imagine if you were out with male friends and a football game started on the television. You then start yelling at the players and the referee, shouting profanities and drinking beer with all the men. Although there's nothing wrong with this if you like a good football match, in that moment you become one of the boys, rather than a potential soul mate.

While this is a bit of an exaggeration, these little things add up, especially in the early days of a relationship or when they occur repeatedly over time.

So how can you maintain polarity? The simple answer is behaving in a way that's true to your core energy, which allows a man to behave in a way that's true to his core energy. If you take on the role of the feminine, then acting in a feminine way will allow him to act as the masculine in the relationship, and vice versa.

Let's start by looking at the role of the masculine man, and what he's looking for from a feminine woman to complement this.

All about masculine men	What he wants from a feminine woman
A masculine man is so focused on getting from A to B he rarely takes time to smell the roses.	He loves it when a feminine woman brings his attention to some beauty in the moment – a sunset, a flower or an animal. She helps him see something he may not have seen while in a more focused state of mind.
He wants to make his woman happy. Some men will choose a woman purely for that fact. If he knows without a shadow of a doubt that he can make her happy, it will make him happy.	He wants her to be happy to see him, and to be able to make her smile. If he feels she's too complicated, he may decide it could be impossible to make her happy. He may see her as too big a problem and simply not worth the effort.
A masculine man wants to please his woman and a big part of that is taking care of his family.	He doesn't want to be taken for granted. He wants recognition and gratitude for everything he does to take care of her and their family.
A masculine man thrives on being appreciated and respected. The more he's appreciated, the more he'll want to do.	He loves it when she is appreciative of what he has done, whether that's his work, supporting the family or organising a date night. Because she acknowledges him, he wants to do more.

Chapter 4: Polarity and attraction

All about masculine men	What he wants from a feminine woman
If the masculine feels he can achieve significance and create long-term certainty for his future in his work, he may focus a large percentage of his time there.	He needs to feel supported. If the woman he's with doesn't support him in his journey or if he thinks that the woman or situation is going to hold him back from his vision, he may leave.
He is afraid of not being enough.	He wants respect and admiration from a feminine woman to reaffirm his sense of self.
He is afraid of not being able to control the situation.	He wants to lead. He wants to take care of her. He doesn't want to be constantly challenged.
He is strong, hard, focused and driven. Because of this, he rarely takes the time to relax and enjoy life. He can be overly serious.	He is attracted to her vulnerability and her softness. When she's fun and carefree, she helps him feel young and happy. Being around her, he won't feel so serious all the time. He can switch off from the pressures of life.

At its simplest, maintaining polarity is about filling each other's gaps – the masculine fills the feminine's gaps, and the feminine fills the masculine's gaps. She is soft where he is hard, she is fun and free where he is serious and determined, and she is in the moment when he is planning for the future.

Banish The Bitch And Bring Out The Babe

The way masculine and feminine energy come together in their differences is by feeling and giving love.

Give him time to miss you

Men like the thrill of the chase, whether it's in sport, at work or with women. However, these days, most women don't let the man do the chasing. Most women will count to ten and, if the guy hasn't called her, she'll call him. That's very masculine.

Letting the guy chase you allows him to be in his masculine energy, which gives you the freedom to be in your feminine energy. It's also a good test of whether he really likes you. If he doesn't call you, he may not be serious. If he doesn't chase you, he's probably not that into you.

When you first meet a guy, if you really like him and he sends you a text message… Wait. Don't reply straight away. Give him time to think about you. Give him time to miss you. If you reply immediately, he's going to think that you've been waiting for his text or that you had nothing better to do. At least wait a few hours.

Once the relationship progresses, if you normally text back quickly, wait a little while with some texts. If he's used to having you text back quickly and it changes, he will wonder why. Let him miss you.

When you do text back, don't feel the need to tell him your whole life story, as then there's no need for him to call. When you do text or email him, make your responses short and sweet. This creates a mysterious aura about you. You're not hiding things from him, but you are leaving him wanting to know more.

Similarly, don't drop everything to go and see him at a moment's notice. He will then expect you to do that all the time, thinking you have nothing better to do. Don't let him think that you are relying on him for your social life and that you're not in demand. Make sure that you have your own life, and that your time is of value. If he wants to be a part of it, he will treat you with respect by organising times with you with enough notice. If he is busy with his life, make sure you're busy with your life. Don't sit around waiting for him. Too often, women put their lives on hold for a man.

Don't try to turn your man into a woman

Problems sometimes eventuate in relationships because each energy type wants the other to be more like themselves. The feminine wants the masculine to be more like her. She wants him to express his inner feelings, she wants him to talk about how he feels, and she wants him to pay her more attention. She basically wants him to act like her. She wants him to validate her feelings. She wants to try to get him to *feel* how she is feeling... or at least understand and have empathy. She is always seeking to be understood.

In the same way, the masculine also wants her to be more like him. He wants her to be focused on their intimate relationship and he wants her to be less emotional.

Both need to realise that each is different.

Feminine energy thrives on love and connection. Because of this, feminine women can spend a lot of time thinking about those they love – their men, their children, their friends and their families. Our man has our focus for a great deal of the time, which is why we would also like to know that he is thinking about us. (This need increases when we are feeling insecure and uncertain.)

This is why it's so upsetting when he doesn't text you, call you or contact you somehow.

In most cases, though, he isn't choosing to avoid you – you're simply not on his mind.

Unlike a feminine woman, a masculine man thrives on success, respect and admiration. To achieve that success (and the subsequent respect and admiration), he needs to focus on achieving his goals. When he's focused on his goals, he's not ignoring you – he's just not thinking about anything else but his outcome.

When she is uncertain, the feminine likes to retreat to her 'nest' or home where she can feel secure. When we want to unwind and relax, we often want to spend time with those we love. If we're on our own, we might be thinking about our loved ones. The masculine, on the other hand, likes to get away and have his own space in his 'man cave'. A man will withdraw to his man cave to unwind and get

Banish The Bitch And Bring Out The Babe

his thoughts together. When a masculine man wants to relax, he withdraws from the rest of the world. Neither approach is wrong – they're just different.

> *The feminine seeks connection through union, likewise the masculine seeks freedom through disengagement.*
>
> *– Nityananda Das*

Yet because we expect men to act like us, we want them to be thinking about us more. Sometimes we even invent manufactured conversations and story lines that might happen when he *does* call or text. For example, we say, 'I would just love him to ring me and tell me that he thinks I'm fantastic and that he wants to go on holiday with me.' Ultimately, though, all this does is set us up for disappointment, as the poor guy has no idea what we're thinking.

A masculine man is totally busy in his world, oblivious to our feelings. He's hard at work and focused on what he's doing. He's in the zone and he doesn't allow himself to be distracted. Most of the time, he honestly doesn't think to call us. Despite how we may feel, he's not ignoring us; he's just busy.

So, if you get upset when a man doesn't text you or contact you as often as you would like, just keep in mind that it doesn't automatically mean he isn't interested, doesn't like you or doesn't love you.

> *It's said that men only have two emotions: They are either hungry or horny. So if you see a man without an erection, make him a sandwich!*

Should you work with your spouse?

This is a great question and it's something you really need to work out for yourself. It can work, but it's important to consider the following points to maintain polarity.

Chapter 4: Polarity and attraction

If you are working with your man in the same business, my experience is that it's best if you have a vision smaller than your man, or if he has a vision bigger than yours, to maintain polarity.

If you have joint goals within your own company, the other way around the polarity issue is having very clear roles and clear divisions within the company.

Having been in business with two partners, I would only consider working with a partner again if it was his business and I was adding value to help him succeed and to become more successful. He would have to have a track record in the business and be the driving force. It would also have to be impossible for me to become the leader in the business, so we would need to have clear roles.

At the end of the day, you have to weigh it all up. In any case, have business contracts in place to protect yourself as well. (I discuss the importance of protecting yourself more in Chapter 5.)

Rick and Summer have an extremely successful business where they have worked together for a long time. They say that they wouldn't have it any other way. Working together is perfect for them. They fulfil each other's needs at work and they make each other feel loved and respected. He's masculine in the work place and she backs him 100 percent, knowing that he's brilliant at his job. He has his vision, he's awesome at what he does and they both have their set roles.

They flirt with each other a lot at work. She dresses up for him and she makes sure he knows what underwear she's wearing. She says they are both very jealous people, so it keeps them close.

Before they had children, she found she used to worry about work at home, which meant she got more involved in the masculine, decision-making role than she needed to be. Once they had children, though, she became preoccupied with the day-to-day running of the children and could leave more of the business decisions and the worry to him. That helped their relationship immensely.

All in all, working together gives them certainty, significance and they definitely learn and grow together. They are pretty much addicted to working together!

Banish The Bitch And Bring Out The Babe

Quick Tip

Yes, there may be times when the man in the relationship is not in his masculine energy and he fails to make decisions, and you may feel you have to step up to get things done. There will be times where you can't help but go into masculine energy. (In your head, you will be saying something like, 'Make a decision already, for goodness' sake!')

If this happens, decide whether you really need to step in to help, or whether you can just leave it to him. How important is the situation? Is it for your survival?

There's nothing wrong with using masculine energy. However, when maintaining polarity, it's about picking what *must* be done at the time and what energy you want to live in.

Summary

If only I knew then what I know now...

- The energy you live in will determine who you attract as your polar opposite. By knowing how polarity works, you can ensure that who you attract is who you want in your life. If you are feminine in your energy, you will attract a masculine man.

- If you attract a feminine man, he'll expect you to take care of him. He will expect you to be the one who makes the decisions. *You* will be the driving force in the relationship. He will always be looking to you to be strong.

- If your man is doing something for you, like booking a holiday, don't jump in to take over the planning. He will soon lose interest in doing anything for you. Think about it... why would he do anything for you if you just take over?

Exercises

1. Think of five men you know. Based on the personality types described in this chapter, what are their personality types? (They can have more than one.)

2. Think of five women you know. Based on the personality types described in this chapter, what are their personality types? (They can certainly have more than one.)

3. Considering the personality types listed in this chapter, which personality types do you see in yourself? Which could you emulate more often? Which could you leave behind? Be honest.

The Lisa B Show

Remember to subscribe to our podcasts at
www.banishthebitch.com/podcast

Chapter 5: Prepare for the man of your dreams

Sometimes we fall in love with the wrong person, but that wrong person helps us prepare to be with the right person.

We've covered feminine energy, masculine energy, integrating the two and creating polarity in relationships. If you're not already in a relationship, it must be time to find a man! Right?

Not just yet.

On coming out of the other side of the break up with her husband, Corina kept telling herself that it was going to be hard to find a man. When she was ready to search in earnest, she registered herself on a couple of online dating sites and went on a few dates.

After a few months, she realised that, even though there were times she wanted to cry out for Mr Right, she had so many more lessons to learn before she could move on and enter another relationship.

You may have heard that when you are ready, he will find you. While it's hard to hear, especially when we're so used to going after what we want and making it happen in other areas of our lives, it's true. He may already be out there looking for someone just like you. However, you have to do your part, too. You need to prepare for being with the man of your dreams.

This involves looking at your dating and relationship beliefs, getting clear on what you want and becoming who you need to be in order to attract him.

One minute you are happy...

While you are looking for Mr Right, you will feel many emotions. One minute you could be over the moon happy with your single life, then the next minute you could feel like crying in the corner.

You could feel any one of these emotions on any given day:

- **Happy and centred –** You are taking care of yourself. Today, you feel in control, you feel stable and you're at peace. You're happy by yourself. You don't need a man to make you happy. You tell everyone your life rocks!

- **Lonely and accepting –** You may feel lonely today but accepting of the situation. You would like a man to hug, to go out with, to hold you and to be with. You would like a man for companionship.

- **Desperate –** You feel sad, lonely and vulnerable. Something may have happened to trigger your upset. Today, you feel you have voids in your life that you're looking for a man to fill. You want a man... *now*! You're not thinking about whether he's the right man for you; you just want your needs filled. In this space, you may allow yourself to make long-term relationship decisions to fill short-term needs. Be very careful if you feel this way.

- **Anti-man –** Today, you could feel very jaded. You may feel shut down emotionally as you have been through hell with men. You've been hurt and you don't want to hurt anymore. In this state, you may say that there is something wrong with you, or there is something wrong with all men in general.

If you are single, our goal is to get you feeling great.

Chapter 5: Prepare for the man of your dreams

Tackle your relationship patterns

Ellie met Tony at a work function. She really liked him and he seemed nice. However, she was petrified of relationships.

She had been single for a long time and she had a child. She had a lot of girlfriends, her family and she had her work. She had a lot of stability in her life – she knew what was happening today and she knew what was going to happen tomorrow. That was her certainty. All of a sudden, Tony showed interest in her and it scared the life out of her.

She went out to dinner with him and she thought he was amazing. Yet, the next morning, she immediately got on the phone to tell all of her friends about her 'massive' problem. She told everyone that she was freaking out. She told them that she wasn't sure about this guy. Deep down inside, she also knew that she sabotaged relationships. She always had.

She then told Tony she was freaking out. She knew that she had erected massive barriers due to her past relationships. They were all firmly planted for her protection, certainty and for her own security. She felt that she had to have them, because she had had so many other relationships that sucked. She had bad memories.

She also explained to the poor guy that she had these barriers. She made sure he knew that she had a 'significant' problem. And she hoped that he would keep pursuing her.

For a while, he did. He thought he could help her. He saw her as a challenge, so he was okay with her drama. But she kept pushing him away.

Subconsciously, she had determined that if he kept persisting, then he must love her. If he didn't, then she could dismiss him, as he mustn't have been that interested in a relationship with her anyway.

What most of us don't realise is that, in every relationship, we adopt behaviours and beliefs in response to our old partners. If these beliefs and behaviours are negative and get carried from one relationship to the next, it can cause a lot of problems, ranging from bickering to shifting the polarity or even ending your relationship.

For example, if a new partner does something aggravating that your old partner used to do, it could trigger the same destructive emotions, even though *it has nothing to do with your new partner*. It's just a pattern that you keep from the old relationship.

Patterns are created following repeated triggers. Let's say that in your first relationship, your partner drank too much alcohol. He got drunk and promptly fell asleep at every party you attended. This made you feel humiliated, which you hated. It also caused a lot of friction in your relationship with him. After you split up with him, you began a new relationship. On your first night out together, he proceeded to have a few drinks and he fell asleep at the party. You looked at him sleeping and remembered all the times that your first partner put you in the same situation. Suddenly you are enraged, and you take years of anger out on your new partner.

It might not even be the same story. Maybe your new partner was sick and was on medication or someone spiked their drink. However, the situation triggered your old pattern of behaviour, which then raised a red flag for this man who had a lot of potential.

Don't assume that changing your partner will mean your next relationship will automatically be different. You may still have the same negative beliefs and run the same patterns. You might react the same way with your new partner, in certain situations, as you did with the old one. This is why it's important to recognise and deal with your patterns.

Do you have patterns you run in your relationships?

We are now going to discover your thoughts and feelings about relationships. You will also uncover any patterns that maybe causing you to have limiting beliefs or blockages.

Chapter 5: Prepare for the man of your dreams

The great news is that once you identify a pattern, you can't 'unknow' it. It's very hard to keep running a negative pattern without feeling slightly silly.

To get started, consider not only your past relationships but also the relationships around you and how they may have affected you. Ask yourself:

- Are there any relationships in your life that have scared or scarred you? Are you worried the same thing will happen to you?
- Did your parents fight? Do you have negative connotations when it comes to relationships and are you trying to avoid them?
- Did your father or mother not love you as much as you thought they should? Do you find it hard to feel love?
- Did the love of your life leave you? Are you worried it will happen again?
- Did your mother leave you when you were young? Has this affected how you feel about being in a relationship? Has it affected your thoughts about having children?
- Did your father remarry several times? Are you worried you won't be able to commit? Do you see marriage as a waste of time?

Really think about this! Are there issues relating to relationships that you may not have dealt with? Is there any reason that you have subconsciously sabotaged yourself from having a fulfilling relationship? What beliefs may have been created that may be holding you back from falling in love?

Some common negative relationship beliefs include:

- 'I'll muck it up and end up with the wrong person.'
- 'My heart will be broken.'

Banish The Bitch And Bring Out The Babe

- 'I don't think I'll know the real person until it's too late.'
- 'Once he really gets to know me, he might break up with me.'
- 'Total fulfilment is only for a lucky few.'
- 'I'm not good enough.'
- 'I'm worried about the financial ramifications and risks of getting involved.'

If you associate a lot of pain with relationships, in order to change your future story, you need to change the story from the past. Remember that your next relationship is not going to be the same thing. You know more now. You have learnt about men and you have learnt about yourself.

Starting from today, say different things. Tell yourself a different story. Use the following questions and affirmations to begin.

- **When you think about relationships, what goes through your head?** Are you happy, sad, excited or angry? Are you excited at the prospect of a new life with someone? Or do you think there are no good men out there? Do you have similar patterns in other areas of your life?

    Your new positive thought: 'My future is exciting. I am ready for the next chapter of my life. My life is what I choose to make it. I have decided to make my life amazing.'

- **What are you focusing on exactly when you think of relationships?** Do you have an idea of the type of man you are after? Or are you focused on a belief that the right man does not exist? Are you pushing other things out of your life as well?

    Your new positive thought: 'I know in my heart that the right man is out there for me.'

- **What are you saying to yourself?** Are you telling yourself that you are better off single? Are you also settling in other areas of your life?

Chapter 5: Prepare for the man of your dreams

Your new positive thought: 'My soul mate will find me at exactly the right time, when we are both ready.'

- **What metaphors are you using?** Do you say that 'all the good ones are taken'? Do you come from scarcity or abundance in other areas of your life?

  Your new positive thought: 'There are plenty of fish in the sea. There are literally billions of men in the world, and there are plenty of men out there for me.'

- **How do you feel when everything is going great with your relationships?** Do you think it won't last or are you making the most of the situation and enjoying every moment?

  Your new positive thought: 'I am grateful for every single moment. I am happy every single day. I always look for the good in everything and everyone, including myself.'

To delve even deeper, think about similar thoughts and patterns in other areas of your life. Consider whether you are generally positive or negative with your reactions.

Most of us have a lot of negative baggage that we think about ourselves. Have you ever thought any of the following?

- 'I'm too fat.'
- 'I can't lose weight.'
- 'I'm too old.'
- 'I'm not ready for a relationship.'
- 'I'm not smart enough.'
- 'Only people who are happy have a perfect body.'
- 'Only people who are unhappy have a perfect body.'
- 'I'm too ugly.'
- 'My hair is awful.'
- 'That guy is too good-looking for me.'
- 'I don't earn enough money.'
- 'I earn too much money.'
- 'He only wants me for my money.'
- 'He's out of my league.'

Banish The Bitch And Bring Out The Babe

Write down any negative beliefs that come up for you – they might be on this list, or there might be other beliefs that are unique to you.

We all have ingrained beliefs we carry around with us. The problem is, the crappy beliefs make us raise our guard or run away. The danger is that, when you meet a guy, you will pull out your mental file on any past crappy relationships. Then you'll start thinking about you and why you're not good enough (or too good) for him.

Based on these, you start making a range of subconscious judgements that trigger your old patterns in response to everything he does. And all the poor guy did was say 'hello!'

Remember, other people's relationships are not yours. Their experiences are not yours. You can define your own experiences and beliefs.

Again, change your patterns. Always try to catch yourself when you have a negative thought, try to turn it into a positive and remember to look for the good in everything.

When you realise that you are running a pattern, you have the power to change it.

~ *What masculine men say* ~

Terry was financially well off and when he started dating, he was concerned that women might only be after him for his money. So he qualified them like this... he didn't let on to any prospective girlfriends that he had money for a few months. He'd pick them up in an old truck and take them to mid-level restaurants. He'd also say the house he lived in was his mother's. He felt it was a great qualifier that sorted out who loved him for him.

Adopt an abundance mentality

My mother and father were married for over fifty years, and were both so grateful that they got to celebrate their fiftieth wedding anniversary before they passed away.

My mother died of cancer and, the day after her funeral, my father was also diagnosed with cancer. He died three months later. While this was hard, it's understandable. After mum died, I really couldn't see my dad being around without her. Dad was centred, strong and determined. He could make anything out of timber and he could fix anything around the house. My mum was his whole world, and he was devastated that he couldn't fix her. He was a great husband and a loyal man. They would back each other; they would joke with one another. They were perfect for each other.

The reason I'm sharing their story is to demonstrate it's possible to have an amazing, awesome, passionate relationship. There is no reason why you can't have that too.

Live in abundance when it comes to men. Don't think that there's a limited supply when there are approximately 3,477,829,638 men in the world, according to the website Geohive. They come in all shapes and sizes, they are different nationalities, some are single, some are thinking about divorcing, some have just got divorced. And you only need *one* of them!

Come from a place of abundance. Your job is *not* to venture out and find a man who doesn't suit you and try to keep him. Your job is to live in adventure. It's to live in fun and find and meet lots of men and find the man who is right for you. The world is a buffet – don't sit around with an empty plate.

The opposite of having an abundance mentality is being desperate. Desperate women chase men because they worry they won't find anyone else. But, as I discussed last chapter, this attitude is very masculine and will either lead men to think you're easy or cause them to take on the feminine role and let you take the lead in the relationship.

> **'Why does that woman have a boyfriend and I don't?'**
>
> Have you ever found yourself thinking this? I hear single women judging other women all the time. They look at couples and say, 'He's quite good looking and he's with that woman! How come he's with her and I'm still single?'
>
> We need to come from an abundance mentality. Don't worry about what others are doing – remember that there are plenty of men out there who will be a match for you.
>
> If you start to doubt yourself, you need to remember this and repeat it over and over – 'When we are both ready, my soul mate will find me.'
>
> Before we attract the right man, sometimes we have things we need to learn. We may need to have certain experiences in order for things to fall into place.

Get clear on what you want

Have you taken the time to think about what you really want in a man, or have you just settled for whoever's shown some interest?

Or perhaps you *have* thought about what type of man you want, only to realise later that you need to adjust what you thought was important after a relationship *you thought you wanted* went sour.

Quite often, people move on from a horrible relationship to another partner, only to discover that they are in *another* crappy relationship. They attracted a similar partner for a number of reasons, one of which is that they didn't have a clear vision of who they were looking for when they started dating. So when they found someone familiar; it felt like home.

Chapter 5: Prepare for the man of your dreams

By knowing what you want, not only will you be more likely to find Mr Right, but you'll be able to avoid men like any past Mr Wrongs.

What are you looking for in a man?

Circle the qualities you want in your ideal partner. Prioritise – what's a must-have and what's a nice-to-have?

- Masculine
- Strong
- Centred
- Emotionally stable
- Funny
- Happy
- Healthy
- Fit
- Strong chemistry
- Eats healthy
- Knows his vision
- Sensitive
- Tries to understand me
- Successful
- Strong presence
- Loyal
- Honest
- Love bug
- Good communicator
- Loves kids or wants kids
- Loves to travel
- Likes my friends and family
- Not jealous but wants me to be his
- Sexy/great lover
- Caring and he *loves* me
- Romantic
- My soul mate
- Knows how to handle me
- Loves to dance
- Intelligent
- Classy
- Cultured
- Well-dressed

Add any other qualities that are important to you that are not on this list.

Then, circle what you won't stand for in a partner.

- Smoking
- Violence
- Cheating
- Lying
- Disrespectful
- Abusive
- Drinking
- Drug addiction
- Moodiness
- Pressures me into doing things I don't want to do
- Belittles me in front of people
- Rudeness
- Possessiveness
- Domineering
- Neglectful

Once you have a list of the qualities that are important to you, as well as the ones you won't stand for, use them as the starting point for a description of what your relationship with this man would be like.

Relationship manifestations

I'm with my soul mate – the man of my dreams.

He's centred, masculine and he's extremely comfortable within himself. He's intelligent and fun. He knows who he is and what he wants.

We allow each other to be our own person. We're honest in our communication and we always reassure each other of our love. We try to understand how the other is feeling. We have fun, we talk and we laugh. We talk about fun things we're going to do together.

He allows me to be feminine. He loves to take care of us and our family. He has a vision, he knows his purpose and he has goals for our life together. He makes me feel like he loves me more than anything else in the world. He loves me for me. He loves and accepts my children

Chapter 5: Prepare for the man of your dreams

and he appreciates that we have an extremely close bond. He never jeopardises these relationships.

I respect him for what he wants to achieve and he respects me for what I want to achieve. I love that he's strong and he knows what he wants. I also respect his bond with his family and friends.

We're addicted to each other and we're addicted to making each other happy. We do romantic things and we surprise each other with gifts. We go on awesome holidays and we spend quality time together. We can't wait to hold each other and we make love for hours. When we look into each other's eyes, we have an amazing connection.

I'm in love with him and in love with life. We wake up every morning bouncing out of bed. After all, that's what life's about.

This is an example of a relationship manifestation, which demonstrates just how clear you can get on the type of man you want to attract and the type of relationship you want to manifest.

Focus on what you want

Now I would like you to write your relationship manifestation. When writing yours, the key is to focus on what you want.

If you're familiar with the law of attraction, you'll know that we attract what we focus on, whether we are thinking about it or feeling strongly about it. If you're bitter about how your last boyfriend cheated on you and you have the attitude that all men are cheaters, you're more likely to attract another cheater. By contrast, if you've let it go and you're looking forward to meeting a faithful and loving man with optimism and excitement, you're more likely to attract what you *do* want.

Additionally, if you keep repeating that you don't want to be single, you may find yourself in a relationship quickly, but because your emphasis was on finding someone fast rather than finding the right person, he may not be Mr Right.

In NLP, we call this an 'away motivation', because you're focusing on what you want to move away from (what you don't want) rather than

Banish The Bitch And Bring Out The Babe

what you want to move towards (what you do want). If you change your thinking to 'I am going to find the man of my dreams', your brain and the universe will start looking for him.

Here are some tips for writing the right manifestation:

- Use positive language, focusing on what you do want rather than what you don't want.

- Use the present tense, as if you already have the man of your dreams. If you use the future tense, your perfect man will always be in your future and will never come into your present.

- Focus on how it *feels* to be with this man. When you write it, and when you read it back to yourself, let yourself feel those emotions.

I still get butterflies even though I've seen you a thousand times.

♀ Visualise yourself in your ideal relationship

Take a moment and go into your heart. Take a deep breath. Think about what your dream man may look like. Is he short or tall? Is he dark or fair? Is he smiling or is he serious? How do you look together?

What do you do with him? Where do you go out? Do you go to the movies or out for dinner? Do you laugh a lot together?

Picture your ideal life. Where would you live? Would you have children? Would you have fur babies?

Chapter 5: Prepare for the man of your dreams

> Try to picture exactly what your relationship would look like. I want you to feel what it would feel like. I want you to smell it. I want you to hear it.
>
> Once you get clear, I want you to write a short story – this will be your relationship manifestation. This will be how you see your future life with him. Your story will be stated in the positive like it has already happened.

Who do you need to become?

Mary is generally a very outgoing, fun girl to be around. Newly single following a traumatic separation, she went out with friends one night and saw the most handsome man she had ever seen.

They glanced at each other across the room. Her heart skipped a beat. Her nerves rose. She folded her arms and she looked away.

What do you do when you are attracted to a man and he makes eyes at you, or he starts talking to you? Do you smile and start talking back, or do you freeze as that little voice kicks in and says, 'Who do you think you are? You're not good enough for him!'

That self-doubt can easily stop you from connecting with your Mr Right.

A big part of your self-belief and self-doubt comes down to the patterns and beliefs I discussed earlier. That said, a massive thing you need to focus on is who you have to be to attract this man.

I've already discussed that masculine men are attracted to feminine women, but there is much more to it than that. If you want someone that makes health and fitness a priority, they would probably want someone who values the same things. So if you need to lose thirty kilos and stop smoking, you're probably not going to attract that kind of man. Similarly, if you're looking for someone who's financially stable, are your finances in order?

Banish The Bitch And Bring Out The Babe

I'm not saying you need to be perfect to attract the man you want, but if you want a catch then you should expect to become a catch yourself. Even if you just start taking steps in the right direction, you'll be much closer to finding the man of your dreams.

Go through the list below and circle who you would have to be to attract your ideal man.

- Feminine
- Honest
- Loyal
- Trustworthy
- Funny
- Healthy
- Great communicator
- Beautiful on the inside
- Centred
- Chemistry
- Sensitive
- Love bug
- Love kids
- Love to travel
- Not jealous but I want him to be mine
- Sexy
- Happy
- Fun
- Flowing
- Confident
- Respectful of his masculinity
- Caring
- Romantic
- Secure
- Intelligent
- Classy
- Cultured
- Well-dressed/well-presented

Add any other qualities that you think your ideal man would be looking for.

By becoming this woman, you'll find your self-doubt naturally starts to fade.

♀ Anchor to your feminine energy – Connect to your feminine energy.

Clench your left fist. Feel every word whilst you read the section below.

If you have one of our *Banish The Bitch* bracelets, wear it on your left wrist. Feel the bracelet acting as an anchor and allow it to store and remind you of the feelings below.

If you need to feel these feelings throughout the day, simply clench your left fist or wear your bracelet on your left wrist to re-establish your anchor.

When you meet a man, make a conscious effort to switch into your feminine.

If you do have a nervous moment, do the following:

- Go into your heart not into your head.
- Take a deep breath.
- Remember that just because someone is talking to you, it doesn't mean you are going to marry them. You're just talking.
- Talk to them like they are your friend – remember to smile!
- Pretend (in your head) you want to get to know him for one of your friends. This takes the pressure off you.
- Communicate from your heart.
- Silently remind yourself that you are beautiful, sexy, irresistible, feminine and everything else he might be looking for. You've already done the work. You have courage, certainty and confidence.

Banish The Bitch And Bring Out The Babe

- Surrender to your feminine energy and allow him to be masculine.
- If you still get nervous, don't judge yourself – he could still fall head over heels in love with you! If he doesn't then it doesn't matter, because we know there are plenty more fish in the sea.

For my relationships with men to change, I needed to change my relationship to myself as a woman.

– Gloria Ng, *Well Water Woman*

Protect yourself

Before entering into a relationship with Mr Small, I was a successful entrepreneur. I had property plus a large chunk of cash.

Mr Small was a little younger than me at the time; he had virtually no assets and nothing behind him financially. Yet, with him, I finally felt love and connection through sex. I felt alive. Because I had felt asexual for such a long time, I finally felt like a woman.

I was thirty-five years old and I could hear my body clock ticking. I longed for a child. Meanwhile, Mr Small knew that I had assets and money. We had been seeing each other for about a year when, one night, he visited me and put forward an interesting proposal: He said we could help each other achieve what we both wanted and we could build a life together. He said we could have a child, and in exchange I could lend him money to start a business. It felt like a win-win.

After careful consideration, in my extreme desire to first be feminine and second to have a child, I said yes to lending him the money. I wanted to trust. I wanted to let go and not be fearful. I wanted to be

Chapter 5: Prepare for the man of your dreams

feminine and I wanted to help him. And I wanted a baby more than anything.

Then everything fell apart.

I loved Mr Small, but I realised that I loved him for the wrong reasons. I loved him for who I thought he could become, and the things he promised, not who he was. I saw him as a project, and I started doing things that I thought would make him more masculine and me more feminine.

I gave him control of my money. I had property that I owned outright, so I organised a mortgage on my house and signed the funds of a re-draw facility over to Mr Small, which was quickly maximised, leaving me with a massive debt on my property. After my parents passed away, I also gave him my inheritance to use for the business.

Everything was lost through the business. Those bad decisions cost me personally well over $600,000.

I found myself with our child, a maxed-out loan and no cash. I felt paralysed.

Before Mr Small, I had always made smart and extremely profitable decisions regarding money. With Mr Small, I made decisions with my heart instead of my head.

Please learn from my mistakes. Take measures to protect yourself. Yes, part of being feminine is surrendering control, but you need to protect yourself in the process.

You should never surrender your intellect for a man. Just because you are going into a relationship, it doesn't mean you forget about your street smarts and your intelligence.

This is particularly important in two areas – financially and sexually.

Money is crucial for our sense of security and survival. It's what pays for our food and our shelter, as well as giving us the freedom to enjoy life. If you lose your money or lose control of your money, it can leave you feeling very insecure and vulnerable.

Because of this, it's important to be very careful of relying on a man to take care of you financially. Depending on what kind of man he is, he could use his financial 'power' to control you. He could threaten to take your security and certainty away at any time. If things turn sour, without money behind you, you could find yourself trapped in that relationship.

If you have money or assets going into a relationship, you have to protect yourself financially. Use smart thinking – get a pre-nuptial agreement, a binding financial agreement or ensure you have business contracts drawn up. Moving forward, this allows you both to have peace of mind and certainty. It takes the guesswork out of your past and opens up your future.

The second area where you need to protect yourself is sexually.

A common dating question is when you should sleep with a man. This is a decision for you as an individual, but I believe it's important to have boundaries for a number of reasons. First, while connecting with someone sexually can be comforting and can ease your loneliness, it can also lead to you forming an emotional bond with a man before you're sure about whether he's Mr Right (or has the potential to be Mr Right). As a woman, the man literally enters your world. The hormone oxytocin is then released in your system, which creates physical and emotional attachment, making it hard for a woman to have sex with a man and not feel strongly connected to him.

Once you've built that connection, it can often come as a surprise that the man doesn't feel the same way. In fact, sleeping with him early in the relationship could have the exact opposite effect as he might think you are easy and desperate.

Second, on a physical level, there are risks when having sex with anyone, including pregnancy, aids and other nasty diseases. Because of this, one of your boundaries should always be asking him to wear a condom. One night of sex is not worth your life.

For these reasons, before you engage in a sexual relationship, work out your boundaries. Set high standards for yourself regarding whom you sleep with and when. Some people wait until they are sure they are in a relationship, others are comfortable sleeping with a man straight away and others will wait until they're married. The key is doing what's right for *you*.

Summary

If only I knew back then what I know now…

- Beliefs and patterns adopted from your past relationships and the relationships around you may be influencing your relationships today. If you want your future to be different from your past, it's essential to address these.
- There are billions of men out there, thousands of whom could be a wonderful match for you. If it doesn't work out with one guy, know there are plenty more where he came from.
- Don't enter into a relationship just because you don't want to be alone. If being alone worries you, get a cute dog or make some new friends. Don't settle. Relationships are too painful when you're unhappy. You are much better off being alone than being unhappy with the wrong person. (And dogs are a whole lot less expensive long-term.)
- If you have money or assets when entering into a relationship, and your partner doesn't, get a pre-nuptial agreement or a binding financial agreement. If you lend them money for a business, have a business agreement completed by a lawyer.
- Never, *ever* get a tattoo with your man's name on it. No matter how much you love them. If you have such a tattoo and you've separated, if you have a child, change the tattoo to your child's name.

Exercises

1. Whom do you want to attract? Breathe into your heart and feel. Picture vividly what this man might look like. Think about:

    a. What features and qualities do you want in a partner? What values are important to you? Honesty, sense of humour, loyalty and so on.

    b. What physical features do you like? Short, tall, dark, healthy and so on.

    c. What features or qualities will you definitely *not* tolerate in a partner? Abuse, violence, smoking, eating meat if you are a vegetarian, jealousy and so on.

2. Who do you have to be to attract this person? If you want a masculine man, are you feminine? If you want a Greek God with a picture-perfect body – will he be attracted to you? If you would like a well-dressed professional and you wear T-shirts and track pants everywhere, would he be interested in you?

Chapter 6: Enter the dating game

It's okay to be nervous. It's okay to put yourself out there. You need to open up, love and learn and then maybe you might need to do it all over again.

When you are ready, you must have the courage to start dating.

Yes, it can be scary, but what will happen if you don't do this now? What will it cost you? The worst-case scenario is that you will be the same as you are now.

Stop feeling sorry for yourself and stop playing those old stories in your head – you know the ones: 'I'm not pretty enough', 'I'm too fat', 'I'm too old', 'I'm too set in my ways', 'I'm not ready for a relationship right now'…

While you may think these stories are protecting you from being rejected by men, the opposite is actually true – you have rejected yourself first. You have stopped yourself from meeting your soul mate. You have stopped yourself from experiencing love and connection with a man.

It's time to put yourself out there and find your knight in shining armour. Just think about the possibility and the excitement of meeting the man of your dreams. The person you want to grow old with. The person who lights you up every time you see them. Someone you can laugh with. Someone you can love, who'll love you more than anything.

But where should you start? Don't worry – that's what this chapter is for.

Fish where the fish are

The first step when you start dating again is to go where the men are. So where might your ideal man be?

This will depend what type of man you want.

My advice is to go where your passion lies; go where the men will have similar interests to you. For instance, Lorri is a dancer whose ideal man is someone who is muscular, fit and athletic. If she wanted to meet this type of guy, she could go to health food shops, dancing nights, gyms and so on.

Here is a sample list of places where you can meet men:

- Gyms
- Coffees shops
- Grocery stores
- Laundromats
- Book clubs
- Dating clubs – Internet sites
- Internet meet-ups
- Seminars
- Shopping centres
- Football games
- Hockey games
- Any sporting events
- Dancing lessons
- Food stores
- Dog parks
- Through friends
- Social media
- Anywhere!

A lot of single women say that one of the best places to meet men is online and others hate the whole online dating process. Your experience will be different to the next person's. The great thing the online dating world will show you is the abundance of available men. It will show you that not all the good ones are taken.

Some say the difference with online dating is that if you go out to a bar, there will be a mix of men there. Some will be with their friends, some will be with their girlfriends or wives, and some might be looking to pick up. Of the fraction who are looking to pick up, some will want a one-night stand, some will want a casual fling and some will be ready for a relationship. This leaves you in the position of figuring out not only who is available, but who is available *and* looking *and* interested in a serious relationship. Suddenly, your buffet has dropped to just a couple of guys in the room.

Some say that online dating sites are a completely different kettle of fish. You have access to thousands, maybe even millions, of men in one spot. A higher percentage of them could be looking to connect, and quite a few of those looking to connect want a serious relationship. Online dating has completely changed the dating dynamic – rather than feeling like you need to compete for the two or three available guys in the bar, for those that love it, you can sift through hundreds of profiles until you find one that's right for you.

Building attraction

When you find a man you like, your early interactions and dates should focus on whether he is relationship material (more on this later in this chapter) and building attraction between you.

Yes, if you click with someone, there will be a natural chemistry between you. But understanding how attraction works can help you build on what's already there, if you decide a man has potential.

So what attracts a man to a woman? As I've already discussed, polarity is the foundation of attraction. Masculine energy is attracted to feminine energy, and vice versa. When a feminine woman is easy to get along with, happy, flowing and low maintenance, just watch the men flock to her.

On the other hand, if you don't smile, or your arms are folded in front of you, you'll seem closed off to communication. Guys may interpret that you're not interested in them, or interested in a relationship with anyone, which could see you sending away men who have potential.

> **Watch what feminine women do**
>
> Do you know a feminine woman who naturally draws quality men to her? Go out with her one evening and observe her working her magic. Imagine that you are filming a dating documentary, and you need to take mental notes of everything she does. What does she do that you don't do? How does she act?
>
> There's a good chance you'll find that her attitude, words, expression and physiology are all centred in her feminine energy.

Beyond polarity, the other part of the attraction puzzle is building rapport. Rapport skills are essential to any negotiation, in your business or personal life. If you don't have rapport, you have nothing.

Rapport can grow in many different ways, but a simple way to start is with a smile and making eye contact.

A more advanced technique is mirroring and matching the person you are speaking to. You can copy or match the way someone sits, the tone of their voice, their tempo, their volume and their breathing. This can be as subtle as a smile, sitting the same way they are or tilting your head to the side like they do. Mirroring and matching makes the person subconsciously feel connected to you. They feel comfortable with you. They feel like they can relate to you.

If you are an extremely fast talker and you start a conversation with someone who speaks very slowly, they are not going to feel very comfortable talking to you. If you slow down and talk at their pace, on the other hand, they will feel much more comfortable and more connected. The same goes for if you are yelling loudly and they are softly spoken – you probably won't build any rapport at all. If you adjust your tone to match their volume, though, both of you will feel more comfortable with the communication.

Is he attracted to you?

You've been in your feminine, you've been matching and mirroring, and you think you and the masculine man you're dating have a lot of chemistry. But how can you tell if he feels the same way?

Here are some hints that signal a guy might be 'into you':

- He buys both of you dinner if he asks you out.
- He makes another time to see you.
- He remembers things you have told him about yourself.
- He opens the door for you.
- He only has eyes for you when you are with him.
- He's present with you.
- He listens to you when you talk.
- He is genuine in conversation.
- He tries to make you laugh.
- He goes out of his way to make you feel protected and safe.
- The relationship is more than a 2am booty call.
- He wants to spend time with you.
- He includes you in some of his plans.
- He introduces you to his family and/or friends (a lot of men won't do this until they are 100 percent sure about you).

Is he relationship material?

No matter how much chemistry you have with a man, it's essential to make sure everything adds up on paper. Because of this, carefully consider whom you commit to. Remember, there are billions of men out there – you don't need to take the first offer you get.

Yes, being lonely can be a horrible thing. But don't let it force you to jump into a relationship. Really consider, when you find someone, whether he's the *right* guy for you. Make sure that he is not just filling a void. Will he merely stop you feeling lonely? Is he just creating a feeling of love and connection through sex? Do you just want companionship?

That's not how to choose a partner. He will end up driving you insane.

The question you should be asking is: Is he the *right* man for you?

> *If he isn't Mr Right, all you are doing is settling for less than you desire and less than you deserve.*

Don't settle...

There are all kinds of ways that we can settle. Sometimes when we enter a relationship, we settle for whoever we are with at the time, even though we might have voices in our head that alert us. (We might also see sirens with red flashing lights and megaphones that shout, 'WARNING! WARNING! WARNING!') We may even have other people telling us not to be with them… and yet we do it anyway.

This is a recipe for disaster.

So why do we settle? Usually it's because we don't want to be alone. We elect to have the security that any relationship gives rather than holding out for total fulfilment and love. We may have someone who makes us feel certain or loved. Sometimes it seems easier to settle for what we have than to start all over again.

Chapter 6: Enter the dating game

Some other reasons include:

- She feels she's not getting any younger and he's a nice guy.
- She doesn't want to be alone.
- Her body clock is ticking and she wants to have children.
- He's extremely loyal and she thinks that he'll never leave her.
- She thinks he'll make a great father.
- Her family likes him.
- He's financially secure.
- She's hoping he'll help her get over her last relationship.
- She might not find anyone that she likes more.
- She believes she'll grow to love him.
- She's bored.

I even know one lady who married her husband because she didn't have health insurance, he had insurance and she needed new teeth!

A message to my heart:
Please fall in love when I am ready,
Not when I am lonely.

When Charlene decided to find a husband, for instance, she told herself she would marry and have children with the next man she dated. Luckily, the very next guy she dated asked her to marry him, and that's what she did. They had three children and they divorced twenty-seven years later. Why? They had no polarity, and they hadn't for many years.

Even though Charlene heard metaphoric alarm bells and fog horns and saw flashing lights pointing to the potential dangers of being with this man, she progressed with the relationship. She chose to accept the warnings, thinking that she could either fix them or she could live with them. But while she had a great life with her children, she lived a miserable twenty-seven years with the wrong man.

You can't commit to someone on the assumption that you'll be able to fix what isn't working. You'll more likely feel pressure to start playing on his level.

Karen is well-educated, she has travelled extensively and she has her own successful companies. She's been educated in business and in life. Prior to Andrew, she had massive goals and aspirations.

Karen felt that she 'punched below her weight' with Andrew. She felt awful for judging him like that. To put it bluntly, Andrew was a lot less intelligent than she was and Andrew made her feel smart. Being with him made her feel good about herself again. He also made her feel alive through sex. While this may seem harsh on poor Andrew, it was a fact.

She met Andrew when she was feeling down. She had low self-esteem and she didn't feel good about herself. She felt she would never fulfil any of her dreams. She felt that being with Andrew was as good as she was going to get. Even though they virtually had nothing in common outside the bedroom, she knew he loved her. She decided that she was okay and settled for love and connection.

However, after being with him for about eighteen months, she felt like parts of her were dying. Her brain felt deprived. He didn't make her feel intellectually stimulated.

After a period of time, she sought to grow again. She started to come alive in her business mind. And he hated it.

Having a partner like Andrew could go one of two ways for Karen, should she become successful. He could operate from love or fear. If he operated from love, he would show support, maturity and trust. If he was masculine and confident in himself, he could handle her success and allow her to shine. If he operated out of fear, however, he could show resentment and jealousy and he could feel out of control. He could try to sabotage her efforts. He could be fearful that she would grow apart from him. He could feel very insecure in himself.

He might not have the skill set or maturity to handle her success. Her success could make him feel emasculated.

Lots of emotions come into either scenario, depending on how each person shows up.

While there are many dangers in this, the first of two very real problems is that, if you 'punch below your weight', depending on his self-confidence and maturity, you may never feel free to soar. You could always be worried about intimidating him or being more successful than him. You may hold yourself back from achieving your dreams. If, on the other hand, you do decide to take off and leave him behind for your career or life's calling, this could very quickly change the polarity in your relationship.

So please choose your relationships wisely.

Don't settle for anyone that you're not sure about. If you're not sure, you're not sure. If you have any doubts, it's a 'no'. Just wait. Don't get married to someone unless you feel a resounding 'yes!'

This becomes even more important when you're thinking about having a child.

I think that sex education classes at school should talk about the consequences of whom you choose as the father of your child. If the father of your child is an asshole, they can influence the decisions you make for your child for decades. Even if you separate, for as long as they are involved in your child's life, you will have to communicate with that person.

If you have a child with someone who doesn't care about you or the child, they might make decisions out of spite and jealousy. They might not let your child travel on holidays to overseas destinations. They could stop you giving your child the best life they could have. If your main priority is making the best life for your child and the other parent's interest is to undermine everything you are trying to do, it can be devastating.

They could also influence your future relationships.

Banish The Bitch And Bring Out The Babe

Test whether he's a match for you

It's important to test each stage of a relationship. If it's okay, you can move on to the next stage.

Imagine walking across a stony creek or waterway. In this creek, there are rocks strategically placed for you to step on. To be safe, you need to take one step at a time and make sure that each step is stable. The same goes for finding the right person for you.

You don't need to rush. Always look for signs that everything's okay.

Take the time to consider whether the person you are seeing is really the right person for you.

First, try to stay impartial. Go out and have a great time, but don't let your emotions get in the way before you know he has potential. Ask yourself: Does he have a similar maturity level, similar values and a similar outlook on life? You need to have things in common.

Second, does he want the same things as you do? If the man is masculine and he knows what he wants, he also knows what he doesn't want. He may say he doesn't want a relationship. He may have certain things he wants to achieve before he settles down. While he may change his mind on those things down the track, he also may not. If you want something and he doesn't, don't expect him to change.

Third, if you notice something that doesn't sit well, take that as a warning sign. If it happens more than once, he might not be the right guy for you. If the relationship doesn't feel right, don't stay there in the hope that it will turn into something else – this rarely happens.

Fourth, take the time to consider whether you actually *like* the guy. So many women focus on trying to attract the guy, trying so hard to make them like them that they forget to consider whether *they* like the guy in the first place.

Warning – Don't take your testing too far!

A woman will test her man all the time. Most women will not even realise they are doing it.

However, there's a difference between testing a man to clarify whether he is a good match, and continually making him jump through hula hoops to ease your insecurity. Just think of Ellie and Tony, who I mentioned last chapter.

How many relationships have you lost because you've made a guy jump through too many of your hoops?

Some people, as soon as they have something good in their life, turn it into a drama. If this sounds like you, it's time to make the decision. You need to decide to stop being a drama queen!

Stop making the poor guy jump through a million hoops to get to you. Know that, if you are playing games, rather than genuinely scoping him out, he won't put up with your bullshit forever.

Sometimes, if they get bored, people create drama in their lives. After all, it's exciting and constantly leaves them in suspense. A woman might also believe it to be a benefit when it comes to not letting anyone get close.

There comes a time in her life when she needs to let go of any drama. A time when she needs to focus on creating the best life she can.

If this is you, it's time to decide that life is about you; it's not about putting on a show for everyone else.

Don't make a man your project

Before committing to someone, think about whether you really like him (or, further into the relationship, whether you really *love* him). Then ask yourself why.

Love a man for who he is, not what he has or what he could be.

Similarly, if you think he's great the way he is, but he could 'fix' a certain area of his life, you might be surprised to discover that he doesn't care about fixing it. You might try to support him and encourage him to fix the 'faulty' part, thinking that with a little bit of your coaching, you can make him perfect! You might suggest that he books into certain seminars, you might apply for jobs on his behalf, or you might encourage coaching or ask him to talk to other people who could help him. The fact is, though, if he doesn't have a personal desire to improve in that area, he probably won't.

This man is his own person. There's a great chance that he won't see that he needs 'fixing'. After all, if he wanted to change, *he* would have orchestrated it. If there's going to be lasting change, he needs to facilitate it. You can try and inspire him, but you can't make him change. Change needs to be *his* choice.

If you want to find a masculine man who is successful and empathetic, you must find a successful, empathetic man to begin with. If he's masculine but not in touch with his feelings, you may find you can help him see what it's like to live in love, fun and adventure.

On the other hand, if you find a sensitive man who's in touch with his feelings, chances are you will not influence him to be confident, strong and successful. He must want to become this himself.

> *Men marry women with the hope they will never change. Women marry men with the hope they will change. Invariably they are both disappointed.*
>
> – Albert Einstein

The moral of the story is: Don't buy a dog and hope that it turns into a cat. Just find a cat. By the same token, if you do want a relationship that you can control – buy a puppy!

Becoming 'exclusive'

When two adults have been dating for a little while, invariably the 'Are we exclusive?' question arises in one way or another.

I understand…

All she wants to know is how he feels about her and if he is seeing anyone else. When we meet a guy, we assess if we like him and if

Chapter 6: Enter the dating game

we can see a future with him. Guys, on the other hand, are simpler creatures. They are only thinking about enjoying our company. (Oh, and they are probably wondering if they are going to get laid...)

Some women will ask a guy after a month or so (sometimes earlier) whether they are exclusive. In the very early days, this can put way too much pressure on him to decide. He may have just left a committed relationship and, to him, it seems like she is asking him to commit to her straight away. Even if he has no intention of sleeping with anyone else, he's not ready to voice his commitment to her either. It's like she's saying to him, 'Can you tell me that you are never going to sleep with anyone else ever again?' This is not the best way to ask.

This can often be exacerbated with online dating, as it's not unusual to be curious about whether a guy is still communicating with other women online. If he is, it can feel threatening and daunting... after all, if he's still registered on dating sites, he's effectively still on the open market.

So what should you do?

Let's start with what you *shouldn't* do, and that is give your man an ultimatum. That's if you're not ready to deal with his potential answer. Ultimatums, in the early days, are a quick way to crash and burn a relationship that could have gone somewhere. Ultimatums are by far the quickest way for the feminine to take on the masculine energy in a relationship, or to prematurely end a relationship that had potential. Men are not like women. They generally do not think about getting married to someone from the beginning of the relationship and they do not constantly think about how they can get a girl to commit to them. Most of them are happy to take things day by day.

If you push your need for a commitment, if he feels that you are giving him an ultimatum and if you try to force the issue, it could go a different way than you hope. If he isn't ready to say 'yes' yet, then his answer will most likely be 'no'. While you will have forced him to make a decision, he might have made a different decision (a 'yes') if he'd been able to do it in his own time.

By the same token, some people feel they would rather just cut to the chase and give their partner an ultimatum. You might feel you need and want to do this for your sanity and your peace of mind. After all, when you have a 'yes' or a 'no' about the future of your relationship, you can plan and move forward. When your life is full of 'maybes', there will always be uncertainty.

If you aren't prepared for the consequences of separating, you may need to learn to take the relationship day by day. After all, what's the rush? If you force him into a corner, he's not going to be as excited, as happy and as enthusiastic as he would have been were it his idea and his timing.

The alternative to ultimatums

So if you shouldn't be giving ultimatums, what should you be doing?

Simply, don't rush for a commitment. Committing to a relationship before you're sure whether you're both ready is a recipe for heartache. You don't want to get too serious before he does. By contrast, in the initial stages of being together, keeping yourself open to dating other men is one way to take the pressure off, and to stay in your playful, free-flowing feminine energy.

Take Marie, for example. Marie had only been dating Steve for a few months. They had never had the 'are we exclusive' discussion. After she started dating Steve, another guy she liked asked her out. She didn't want to say 'no' if Steve wasn't serious.

She told Steve, 'I really like you and I need to tell you that I've been asked out on a date. Do you think I should go? I'm really not sure if you would like us to be exclusive?'

If he said that he didn't want her to date anyone else, then that would show her he wanted the relationship to be exclusive. If he said 'yes', then it would be a confirmation that he didn't think of them as an exclusive couple (yet).

Marie could continue enjoying her time with Steve while meeting other men, any of whom could be her Mr Right.

How you do this in your relationships is up to you. Some women are happy to date different men at the same time, but won't sleep with any of them until they are exclusive. Other women will have an ongoing relationship with someone and will sleep with him, but will continue dating others on the side until their exclusivity is confirmed. This is up to your morals and how you feel.

One of the benefits of dating several people before your preferred man commits is that you will have a thriving social life and a busy calendar outside your time with him. This will then make him realise that you are in demand and he can't expect you to be available at the last minute – he will need to book dates with you in advance.

If you feel uncomfortable with dating a number of people, instead, just keep your life full with your friends and interests, rather than getting overly attached to the man you're seeing before you commit to each other.

If you have your profile on dating sites, another thing you could do is leave it on there until he asks you to take it off or you have the discussion regarding your exclusivity. It doesn't mean that you have to date other people (though you can if you want to!). It just means you haven't pinned all your hopes on someone too early.

Don't be a bitch about it

Out of frustration to move to the next level, some women make up stories about potential suitors.

Don't make up stories about other guys asking you out to test him. (Unless you want to piss him off.) It will come across as a threat. It will sound like you are saying that if he doesn't want you, you have others lined up. It will make him wonder if you are 'girlfriend material' and if you really like him. It can feel like, unless he does what you want, you would quite happily swap him for someone else.

Just be honest. If someone else does ask you out, this can be an opportunity to open a conversation about exclusivity. If they didn't, don't pretend they did.

Banish The Bitch And Bring Out The Babe

Dealing with rejection

Not all relationships are meant to be and, at some point, all of us experience rejection. When you are with someone you like and they don't feel the same way, it hurts. If you build up enough courage to tell someone that you like them in that way and they don't reciprocate your feelings, it can be devastating.

After my mum died, a friend sent me a beautiful email that I keep in mind when relationships end.

> *People come into your life for a reason, a season or a lifetime.*
>
> *When someone is in your life for a* **REASON,** *it's usually to meet a need you expressed. They have been sent to assist you through a difficult time, to provide you with guidance and support, to aid you physically, emotionally, or spiritually. They may seem like a God-send, and they are! They appear for the reason you need them. Then, without any wrong-doing on your part, or at an inconvenient time, this person will say or do something to bring the relationship to an end. Sometimes they walk away, sometimes they die. Sometimes they act up and force you to take a stand. What we must realise is that our need has been met, our desire fulfilled and their work is done. What you have asked for has been answered, and now it is time to move on.*
>
> *Some people come into your life for a* **SEASON,** *because your turn has come to share, grow, or learn. They bring you an experience of peace, or make you laugh. They may teach you something you have never done. They usually give you an unbelievable amount of joy. Believe it! It is real! But, only for a season.*

Chapter 6: Enter the dating game

LIFETIME *relationships teach you lifetime lessons: things you must build upon in order to have a solid emotional foundation. Your job is to accept the lesson, love the person, and put what you have learnt to use in all other relationships and areas of your life. It is said that love is blind but friendship is a clairvoyant.*

Thank everyone for being a part of your life – whatever the reason.

Dating and relationship tips

- Don't put a man down with humour, especially in front of other people. It's horrible and no one likes it.
- Don't talk about marriage or kids on the first few dates. If he brings it up, then you can talk about it, but remember that you are elusive and you are definitely not needy!
- Don't whine and complain about everything. He'll think, 'If she's whining now, what would she be like if I married her?'
- On your early dates, don't give him the full saga about why your last relationship ended. Just say that it didn't work out and it's in the past. Later, if he asks, you can tell him.
- When men speak to you, you don't have to reveal too much. You want to come across as a mystery. A girly, happy, fun mystery that he'll want to know more about.
- If he's funny, laugh at his jokes – he'll love it!
- Be feminine and let him look after you. If he gets the door for you, say, 'Thank you.'
- Don't finish his... sentences.
- Do *not* tell potential suitors how many men you have slept with. Trust me on this – you do not want to tell them! It's personal.

Banish The Bitch And Bring Out The Babe

- If you are single and you are out at a club, walk around the room wearing a great big smile to make sure the men see you. You can walk to the ladies' bathroom, apply your makeup or see if your friends have arrived. Anything to let the men know that you are there.

- If you want to attract a masculine man, you should always expect the man to contact you. If he wants to know more about you, he'll do the chasing. At the end of the day, he'll respect you more because he knows how hard it was to get you.

- If you are single, don't tell a man you are 'single' because he'll feel that there's no competition. If a guy asks you if you are single say, 'No, I'm dating.' If he likes you, a masculine man will want to compete to win you.

- When you first go out with a guy, don't drop everything to go and see them at a moment's notice. He will then expect you to do that all the time, thinking you have nothing better to do. Make sure that you have your own life.

- Just because you are asked out on a date, it doesn't mean you have to go. If a guy asks you out, instead of going out for dinner, organise to meet for coffee. This can be a lot less intimidating and it also allows you to make a quick getaway if needed.

- If a masculine man asks you out on a date, he will generally pay for your meal. If you're not sure, you can get your purse out. If he then says that he'll pay, let him! Don't argue. A masculine man will not want to argue with you about the bill. If he wants to take care of you, let him. If he pays for dinner, you can offer to buy drinks, ice cream or something else. If you asked him out, then see what happens.

- If he asks you out on a date and you decide you're not interested in him and you only like him as a friend, I would drop into the conversation that you feel that you could be good mates and then I would insist on paying for your share of the meal. That will give him a big clue that you are not interested in him.

- A masculine man will generally look after women as a group. If you are at a party with your man and there are single women there, you may find that he offers to pay for their meal. He might want to make sure that they get home all right as well. He may organise taxis for them or get someone to walk them to their car. Don't feel threatened – this is what makes him feel needed and masculine.

- Don't necessarily look for Mr Right or Mr Perfect; look for Mr Right Now. Use your intelligence and your gut feeling to determine if you should go out with him. He may not be perfect, but neither are we. Once you go on a date, you can then determine whether he is a possibility.

- Only tell people who support you about your soul mate search! Stay away from negative people.

- When you're feeling uncertain, scared, nervous or just plain fed-up, remember that it's normal to go through these stages.

- If you are interested in a man and you don't know how to tell him, suggest to him that you could do something together. Say something along the lines of, 'Have you been to the Japanese restaurant on High Street? Maybe you and I could go there together some time.'

- If you put your profile online, don't judge your level of attractiveness by whom you attract. I know a twenty-year-old, blonde model who specified she was interested in men from twenty to twenty-five yet was inundated with requests from overweight, bald men in their fifties!

Summary

If only I knew then what I know now…

- Choose your partner with a wise mind and your eyes wide open – you will be way ahead of the majority. You can't commit to someone on the assumption that you'll be able to fix what isn't working.
- When you are both ready, he will find you. He's out there looking now. You have to do your part too. You need to go out to meet people and you need to register on reputable dating sites.
- When you first start dating, don't rush your man towards exclusivity, as you could kill off a relationship before it's even begun. Instead, continue being available for other dates so you don't pin all your hopes on one guy.
- If you feel rejected, remember that people come into our lives for a reason, a season or a lifetime. If someone needs to move on, then they were only there for a reason or season.

Exercises

1. Where will you meet the person you described in the last chapter? If you have identified you would love someone who can dance, get out of your comfort zone, go to dancing clubs or organised dance meetings. If you have identified you want a professional in a certain type of industry, find out where they might be and go and meet some new friends. (Note: You won't meet them in your lounge room. Unless you are registered for online dating.) What do you love to do? Find out where you can meet people who have the same interests.

Chapter 6: Enter the dating game

2. Join some meet-up groups.

3. Even if you are a little shy, register for online dating. Get used to the idea. Make sure you list your interests; be creative.

4. When dating someone new, ensure he passes all the important tests before you commit.

- Does he have a similar maturity level, similar values and a similar outlook on life?
- Does he want the same things as you do?
- Do you actually *like* him?

Help others

If you have a story about your own journey with masculine and feminine energy or you have a relationship story that you think will inspire or empower other women, please tell us!

We are always looking for stories for our website and people to interview in our podcast.

If you feel you could help others, we would love to hear from you.

www.BanishTheBitch.com/tell-your-story

Part 3

You and Him

Chapter 7: Your relationship foundations – How to keep your soul mate

The worst distance between two people is not understanding each other.

Once you and Mr Right are together... Once you have made it through those early stages and have entered a committed relationship with each other, it puts both of you in a fantastic environment for growth, support and acceptance.

Relationships are a place to learn the lessons of loving someone unconditionally, while still allowing each other to remain their own person.

But what happens then? How do you maintain the spark that originally drew you to each other? What can you do when things go wrong? How can you get the spark back? And how do you know if it's time to end it? This is what I'll be covering in the coming chapters.

Banish The Bitch And Bring Out The Babe

The foundations of your relationship

A relationship should be based on trust, respect and vulnerability. It's about letting down your guard and allowing someone to get to know the real you, connecting at the deepest level, voicing your inner thoughts, feelings, fears, hopes and dreams. It's about both of you growing as individuals as well as together.

While relationships are not usually measured, I believe there are some qualities that can be measured to help you see where you stand and pinpoint any problem areas. These include:

- Communication
- Love
- Intimacy
- Aligned values
- Common goals
- Polarity
- Self-love

If you are with a man now, take a moment to grade your relationship on a scale of 1 to 10 in each of these areas, where number 1 means you feel completely unfulfilled and your needs aren't being met at all, and number 10 means you are so fulfilled in that area that you are overflowing.

If you are not with a man as yet, think about each area and envision how you would like each area to be.

- **Communication –** How often did you sit down and talk to each other this week? Did you have a conversation where you were totally present and connected? How often would you like to sit down to talk and connect?
- **Love –** Do you feel loved by the other person? Why or why not? What are your triggers for feeling loved? Does your

Chapter 7: Your relationship foundations – How to keep your soul mate

partner know how they can make you happy? To feel loved, does your partner need to say they love you? Do they need to phone you twice a day? Would you like them to buy you presents? Would you like them to spend quality time with you? Would you feel loved if they made dinner for you? What are your rules for feeling loved? You also need to make sure your partner is feeling loved. Do you know how you can make them feel loved? Love is a two-way street.

- **Intimacy –** Do you and your partner make love regularly? Do you feel loved by them and connected to them? How often would you like to make love?

- **Aligned values –** Do you believe your values are aligned? Is your focus on what's important in life similar? Do you both know what's important to each other? What rules could you relax in order to keep the peace a whole lot more often?

- **Having common goals –** What are your joint goals? Do you want to buy a bigger house? Do you both want to go on a special holiday overseas together? Do you want to help your favourite charity? What are your personal goals?

- **Polarity –** How is the polarity in your relationship? Is there chemistry and opposite energy attraction? Who in the relationship is the masculine energy and who is the feminine energy? What is your energy?

- **Self-love –** Do you have respect and love for yourself? Can you fulfil your own needs, or do you rely on your partner to feel loved? Do you independently communicate with your friends and family? Do you maintain your outside interests?

In this chapter, I'll be discussing the foundations of a relationship – communication, love, intimacy, aligned values and common goals. In the next two chapters, I'll be touching on polarity and self-love in more depth.

Communication

Men simply don't think like women.

This reminds me of a story I heard recently. Kathy and Jack had been dating for four months to the day. When they went out to dinner, Kathy said, 'I can't believe it's July 25th! Hasn't time gone fast?'

Jack looked up in surprise, thinking, 'Shit! The 25th of July is mum's birthday. If I don't call her, I'll never hear the end of it.' He began to think about the consequences of not calling his mother.

Kathy took one look at the horror on Jack's face and thought, 'Wow... obviously he can't believe it's been so long. He must be considering our future. Actually, if he looks like that, he's probably considering ending it. Because he would have known it was our anniversary, and if he was happy about it, he would have *looked* happy about it.'

Meanwhile, Jack was thinking, 'I'm going to have to run to the bathroom and call mum before she calls me.'

Jack excused himself and went to the bathroom to call his mum. He returned shortly after and ate a full three-course meal. He dropped Kathy off at home and then went home and to sleep for ten hours straight.

Kathy stressed and picked at her food all evening. Once she got home, she called all of her girlfriends to tell them that she thought Jack was going to break it off with her, after which she barely slept all night.

Imagine how different Kathy's evening would have been if she had just said to Jack, 'Is everything okay? You look like you're worried about something.'

Communication is everything.

Great communication involves listening to and really feeling what your partner is saying. It's talking about anything from tree frogs to business ideas to world peace. Great communication is being involved in your partner's life. Great communication is wanting to be involved in your partner's life and wanting them to be involved in yours. Great communication reassures your partner.

A lack of communication in relationships is where problems start. If we're too scared to open up or we don't want to rock the boat or we're worried that our partner won't love us anymore, we won't feel safe to share. This is dangerous, because if we never share our problems and concerns, how can we fix them?

Our lifelong partner should be our best friend, our lover and our confidant. Why, then, is letting our partner know how we really feel uncomfortable?

Unless communication has always been an issue for you, in which case it might have more to do with confidence, poor communication is usually a sign that there are problems in the relationship. When we start to have problems, it can become more and more difficult to express our feelings to our partners. We worry that we will hurt them. We're terrified that they will take their love away.

The truth is that there is nothing more reassuring and comforting than knowing that the person you're with allows you to be yourself and allows you to say what you're thinking and feeling without judgement. It feels safe and certain to be in a relationship where you can tell them anything and you have no fear of rejection or loss of love.

But what if you don't feel that way? Then it's time to start communicating differently.

Masculine and feminine communication

We are different in the way we communicate.

Those in their feminine energy are emotive thinkers and those in their masculine energy are logical or literal thinkers. This will affect how you communicate with your man.

The masculine focuses on what they need to do. They either solve the problem or talk about how to solve the problem. Because of this, when they communicate, they will make statements like, 'I'm going to stop for a hamburger,' or 'I'm turning the heater up,' if they voice what they are going to do at all.

The feminine, on the other hand, communicates by sharing the emotion they are feeling. They will say, 'I'm hungry,' 'I'm tired,' or 'I'm cold.'

When a man understands and acknowledges a woman's feelings, she feels like he truly cares about her. When he says, 'Honey, I can imagine how you are feeling right now,' she feels like he gets her. She feels like he's feeling her pain. She feels understood.

When men truly listen to us, we feel a closer connection to them. When we cry and we tell them how we feel, the best thing they can do is put their arms around us and say, 'It will be alright.' We love it when we feel that we have their support. We like to know they have our back. It's very calming to feel understood and protected.

However, masculine men aren't naturally inclined to discuss feelings. When a feminine woman has a problem, a masculine man can find it confusing, as he will always want to try and fix the problem. So he is more likely to say, 'Don't feel like that, fix it like this…' than 'I know how you feel.'

However, often, the feminine just needs to vent, and here's where the problems start. The feminine generally addresses her problems in an emotive way. She will cry and state how she feels. The masculine, on the other hand, is downright baffled by this behaviour. He has no idea how to unravel her emotions and search for the problem. He doesn't know how to calm her down, and he has no idea how to get to the bottom of her issue. For him, it's equivalent to being given a Rubik's cube to solve in three and a half minutes – all he wants to do is solve the puzzle.

It doesn't help that sometimes the feminine gets so caught up in her emotions that she doesn't even know what her problem is. It may take her a little while to work out how she feels and why she is feeling this way. Meanwhile, he's still baffled. He's a logical thinker who tries to take the emotion out of everything so he can make a clear decision.

If this sounds familiar, here's what you can do. First, decide whether you want his help solving a problem, or whether you just want to vent.

Chapter 7: Your relationship foundations – How to keep your soul mate

If you want him to help you solve the problem, try to decipher what the problem actually is. Take some time to write it down and present the problem to your man in writing, in bullet-point form. List each issue individually. He will then have the concept to work from.

This is what my friends husband wrote to her in an email when she was feeling a bit overwhelmed – this would have to be one of my favourite emails of all time!

> *Here is an initial event plan. We will work on and develop this document over the next few days. Then we will build out a timeline and execution plan.*
>
> *No need to feel overwhelmed. I got this!*

She said she was reset. Ahhhh of course she was. Heaven!

If you want him just to listen and to make you feel heard and understood, let your man know. Tell him that all you need him to do is listen to and acknowledge your emotions. Let him know that you don't want him to offer a solution; you just need him to listen to you. For example, if work has upset you, then tell him that. Then you can elaborate by sharing your emotions, such as, 'I feel angry, jealous, insecure, nervous, excited, hurt, sad, happy, supported, loved, proud, disappointed, concerned, confused...' He can then relax, knowing you are simply getting things off your chest – he won't be trying to unravel and decipher your problem.

Know that sometimes when you tell a man your problems, if you don't handle them the way we just discussed, he will take ownership. You need to be careful that you don't express yourself in a way that makes your man take responsibility for how you feel. Again, just let him know it's how you are feeling. You don't want him to fix it; you just would like him to listen. Sometimes when you voice your concerns, he will think either that you want him to help you solve them, or that they are somehow his fault and you're having a go at him. For example, if you tell him that you hate the house that you live in and he's doing his best to provide for you and your family, he may feel upset and feel like he's let you down or disappointed you.

Banish The Bitch And Bring Out The Babe

We are not only different in our communication styles; our thought processes are also different. Masculine energy can compartmentalise much more effectively, whereas feminine energy interweaves every topic together.

If we liken both energies to a computer, masculine energy will only have five Internet browsers open in their mind at any one time. He'll categorise the tabs that are open into groups and will stay in the one tab and focus until the job there is completed. When he is finished, he will close the tab. Feminine energy, on the other hand, will have about 974 browsers or tabs open all at once. She will flick back and forth through the tabs checking to see if all the categories are okay. She'll never close the tabs; she will just minimise them. Her mind never stops. She leaves a trail of unfinished business in her wake.

Helping the masculine share his feelings

When the masculine is free to be himself with his partner, he can experience life to its fullest. If the masculine permanently shelters his emotions from his partner, he'll never get to experience the full spectrum of emotions available in life. When he's with a woman he trusts, he can be real, probably more so than with anyone one else in his world.

This concept may be something completely new to the alpha male. He may have trouble opening up this way and he may only do this on very rare occasions. When he does, give him space and allow him to get his feelings out. When you are in your feminine energy and when he feels your complete trust, he will feel safer opening up to you in time. He will need to feel safe to be vulnerable. You can help by praising his efforts, letting him know he is doing his best. Always reassure him that you are there for him no matter what.

Sharing his feelings and showing his vulnerability doesn't mean he'll constantly complain or always share doubts with his partner. He may just mention his concerns about how he'll attack a situation, he may need to work through the solutions before he talks to her, or he may let her know once he's dealt with the problem. He will most likely want to be certain about his approach before he shares, as he won't want to scare her. He might even fix the problem and share afterwards. He might not even say what he's worried about; he might just say he needs her support or love. Sometimes he just wants to *feel* her love.

However, when he begins to share, this sharing will allow him to grow and evolve by opening up his psyche to a life that feels complete and full.

The only way you can help him to share is to make him feel safe to do so. He needs to trust you with his thoughts. He needs to know you won't throw it back at him later. He needs to know you can handle his truth.

Having the difficult conversations

If you think and feel that there's something important that you need to discuss in your relationship and you're not saying it, you are effectively lying to yourself. You are covering up your own feelings.

In these cases, you have three choices:

1. Tell your partner how you feel.
2. Don't tell them how you feel.
3. Tell someone else or seek some counselling.

With all three scenarios, it's important to weigh up the consequences. What could you comfortably live with?

Can you really avoid talking about how you feel? There's always the risk that if you don't deal with how you feel, it will eat away at you and create negative anchors between you and your partner. You feel a negative emotion when you look at them. Then you feel it again when you look at them. Then, all of a sudden, you look at them and you feel the negative emotion, even though they've done nothing. The longer you let these anchors grow, the more difficult they are to break.

In many cases, it's better to tell your partner and suffer the consequences. Imagine the worst-case scenario – will he get angry at you? Could you break up? Then, compare this to holding the problem you're worried about inside for months or even years. What will your relationship be like if you keep doing that? Would that be worse than the worst-case scenario if you *did* speak to him?

If the likely consequences of speaking out are too high for you (as in, the relationship could end), at the very least, try speaking to a friend or getting some counselling. Getting the issue off your chest could help immensely. You might find that, once you've spoken to someone, you no longer *need* to speak to your partner. Or speaking to someone else might give you some perspective, so you realise that you can speak to your partner after all.

I do have one caveat, as far as honest communication goes. If you want someone to be honest with you, don't ask them a question if you're not going to like the answer. Don't expect them to lie when it suits you. If you're totally honest with your partner, there's a great chance they will be honest with you.

In saying that, there's one exception to this rule where women would *not* like men to tell us the truth… To any men that might be reading this, if your partner asks you the old question, 'Do I look fat in this?' Do *not* tell her she does! If she doesn't look her best, a good answer is, 'Can you try on a few more things and I will tell you what looks best?'

Love

Love is what binds two people together. It's the reason we want to be with that person. However, there are two types of love in a relationship – we can 'love' someone and we can be 'in love' with someone.

In our intimate relationship, our aim is to be 'in love'. There is a difference.

Chapter 7: Your relationship foundations – How to keep your soul mate

When you are 'in love' with your partner, you want to make them happy. You want to spend time with that person. You shine when you are with them and you want them in your future. You want to be intimate with them as an extension of your love. You love them with all your heart and soul.

When you 'love' your partner, you can love them deeply. You love who they are as a person; you just don't love them 'that way'. You feel love but you don't necessarily want to stay with them in the future. You don't feel the desire to be intimate with them. They feel more like your brother or sister, or just a great friend.

> *You need to feel your man's trustable presence before you will open your heart and body without guard. It's a step-by-step process of learning. He learns to be more present, you learn to be more open.*
>
> *– David Deida*

How to feel loved

Clients of mine, Robert and his wife Mandy, had been having relationship problems for some time. She was unhappy, which made him unhappy.

She did not feel loved by him and he couldn't understand why. He texted her every day from work to say that he loved her and he said that he made her dinner once a week. He didn't feel that he needed to do anything else, because in his mind, she didn't need it. He said that *he* didn't need gifts or reassurance to feel loved, so he believed that she didn't need anything else either. He felt that he shouldn't have to 'jump through hoops' to make her feel loved.

He didn't understand that the way he felt loved was completely different to how she felt loved.

Robert needed to decide what kind of relationship he wanted. He needed to decide how happy he wanted to make his wife feel. If he really wanted to keep the relationship alive, then making her feel loved would help their relationship. If his wife were happier, it would also make him happier.

As I discussed in *Communication*, the masculine and feminine think very differently.

Different people also feel love in different ways, though in this case there is more of an individual preference rather than a clear masculine/feminine divide.

In Gary Chapman's *The 5 Love Languages*, he states that there are five different ways in which we give and want to receive love. They are:

- Quality time – The focus is spending quality time together.
- Gifts – The focus is sharing thoughtful gifts or surprises.
- Words of affirmation – The focus is telling your partner how much you admire them and or love them.
- Acts of service – The focus is doing loving acts for your partner, like making dinner, cleaning the house or taking care of the kids. This is simply helping make their life easier.
- Physical touch – The focus is touch, whether that is holding hands, kissing, cuddling or making love.

When you consider the five love languages, which one makes you feel loved? Is it spending quality time together? Does someone have to tell you how great you are and how much they love you? Do they have to buy you gifts? Do they have to make you dinner and wash your car? Do they have to hold your hand and hug you? Do you need intimacy?

Then think about how your partner feels loved. Which of the five love languages do they respond to the most? We tend to give love the way we want to receive it, so also think about how they show their love for you. Before looking at this list, you probably didn't know what your love language is, so how could your partner know? Knowledge is power.

Chapter 7: Your relationship foundations – How to keep your soul mate

> *Men are like dogs. We get excited to see you and we have no idea why you are upset or cranky.*

Love languages in masculine and feminine energy

You will need to be in your feminine energy in order to make your partner feel loved and for it to mean something to him.

Let's say your partner's love language is words of affirmation. If he does something wonderful for you and you say something nice to him in your masculine energy, it will most likely mean nothing to him. For example, if you give him a high five and a slap on the back saying, 'Great job mate,' – it will feel like something one of his friends would do, not something his intimate partner would say.

In order to have any effect, you have to use your words of affirmation in a caring, loving, feminine and sincere way. For example, hold his hand and look him in the eye whilst you tell him how amazing he is and how much you love him. This will produce a completely different result.

There needs to be thought and feeling behind the intention. As you know, you can have all the ingredients to bake a cake, but if you don't follow the recipe, the cake will fail. It's the same thing with your love language; if you don't have the right words and the right energy, it won't work.

> **Learn your partner's love language**
>
> Ask your partner to close their eyes and to think of a time when they felt totally loved. What happened? How did they feel? What was it about that experience that made them feel loved?
>
> Have them share all the details they can remember, as if they are telling you a story. They may say, 'I was seven years old and I went to the movies with my mum and she bought me

Banish The Bitch And Bring Out The Babe

> everything that I wanted at the candy bar.' This particular person felt love through gifts.
>
> Which love language does your partner describe? Did they have to hear the words 'I love you'? Were they touched? Did they receive a gift? Did someone spend time with them? Did someone do something nice for them? This will give you an insight into how you can make them feel loved.

Knowing how someone feels loved is an amazing tool which you can replicate to create more love in your relationship.

Go through the five love languages with your partner, children and family members. Assess what love language they respond to. This will help you to know how to make them feel loved. It's very powerful.

I believe that, in any relationship, every day, you should aim to make your relationship better. That will also make your life better than it was the day before. Make where you live look nicer or organise a holiday to look forward to; do something little each day to improve your life. Here are some ideas to make your partner feel more loved:

- **Spend quality time with your partner.** Make times where you show him how much you love him by making him your number one priority. Organise a special date night and spoil him. It could be a walk along the beach with a bottle of wine; it could be a night at the movies – whatever your partner loves to do. Aim to make his day special.

- **Tell your man how grateful you are for anything they do.** Give specific examples of what you admire and what you are grateful for. Thank him for phoning you. Thank him for helping you with something. Thank him for dinner. Thank him for everything he does. If you think he's amazing, tell him!

- **Let your partner know how his behaviour affects you emotionally.** Say, 'It makes me happy when you include me.'

'I feel loved when you phone me.' 'I feel scared when you drive really fast.' 'I feel sad when you ignore me.'

- **Have fun and laugh!** See the world through the eyes of a young child. Jump in a puddle without thinking about getting your shoes wet. Laugh and have fun. Dive in a pool without feeling the water first – if it's cold, you might not get in. Play games.
- **Inspire him by following your own dreams.** Make sure you know what you want. Become a source of inspiration to yourself. When you're in your flow and you are happy, the right man will find you irresistible.
- **Buy your partner thoughtful gifts.** You don't need an occasion to buy your loved one something that makes him feel loved by you. You may even make him smile. Make it fun and spontaneous. It doesn't have to be expensive – just thoughtful.
- **Touch him more often.** Touch doesn't have to be sexual. Have regular cuddles, stroke his hair, stroke his face and hold his hand when you are walking along. When you go out for dinner, hold his hand.
- **If you need something – ask!** If you need a hug, or if you need something else, ask for it.

Do whatever is important to them – whatever makes them feel loved.

How can your partner make you feel more loved?

Unfortunately, you can't just go to your partner and say, 'I want you to make me feel more loved!' It doesn't work like that – you can't make someone *want* to make you feel loved.

You can share with them what makes you feel loved – you can share the concepts of *The 5 Love Languages*. You can share how you feel with them or you can read through this chapter with them. If you both want to work on your relationship, you can make a plan together.

However, at the end of the day, we can't rely on anyone else to make us feel loved. As I discuss in Chapter 10, we can only rely on ourselves. There are many ways we can feel loved and it's up to us to explore the different sources of love. In any case, the number one source of love is our love for ourselves.

Exercise

1. What is your love language?
2. Think about the three people closest to you, what's their love language?
3. How can you make those people feel more loved?

Intimacy

Connection through love-making is important in any healthy and passionate adult relationship. It's what sets your relationship with your partner apart from a non-intimate one.

A healthy, monogamous sex life sets the scene for a deep connection with your partner. It makes you feel loved and special in a sacred union between two people. It creates oneness and connection that only the two of you get to experience with each other.

Masculine energy is generally more focused on sex than the feminine. Men are biologically wired that way as they have testosterone raging through their bodies. Feminine energy will generally be turned on by the polarity they feel to their man.

Did you ever have a spark?

If you don't have the intimacy you want in your relationship, ask yourself whether you and your partner have ever had a healthy intimate relationship. Have you ever had that spark?

Chapter 7: Your relationship foundations – How to keep your soul mate

If you did, that's a great start – it means there's something you can work with.

The next thing to consider is what changed.

- What were you doing differently to what you do now?
- How do you treat each other now compared to when you first got together?
- Have there been any prior indiscretions?
- Do you have any bad anchors or associations related to him?
- If you do, how much do you want to move past the drama and focus on the future?
- Are you really prepared to put the past in the past?
- If you're not prepared to move on with how you feel, how long are you going to carry those feelings for? A week, a month, a year or forever?
- How will this affect your relationship?

How do you rebuild?

If you see there are cracks in your relationship, if it's important to you, you will need to enter a phase of rebuilding what you once had. You need to make your relationship important. If you don't, you soon might not have a relationship at all. If you have children, you have to organise time alone together. Start with having date nights, time for just the two of you. Make sure the night involves something fun that makes you laugh, scream or get so excited that you can't wait. Plan days where you take a picnic on the edge of the water. Go and see a band you love. Plan a holiday together. Plan things you both really love to do and make sure it's fun.

Do everything you can to make your relationship better. If, after you have tried everything, you're still not sure about your relationship, you might need to separate for a few weeks or months to really gather your thoughts about how you really feel.

If you feel like you and your partner never had a spark, it's time to ask some hard questions:

- Are you honestly with the right person?
- Why did you get with him in the first place? Was it for the right reasons?
- Do you really want to be intimate or are you just going through the motions?
- Are you prepared to do everything to try to make the spark happen and give your relationship the best chance?
- Do you 'love' him or are you 'in love' with him?

If not, it might be time to consider your future.

It's okay to enjoy sex

When you were growing up, you may have been taught that sex was a topic you shouldn't discuss, that it was wrong or that it was dirty. Perhaps it was hidden away.

Yes, some situations can make you feel uncomfortable, there are the seedy sides to sex, and there are horrible people who do the wrong thing. For the purposes of this book, though, I am referring to loving relationships between two consenting adults, which is never wrong.

As adults, when two people love each other and want to express their love, sex is an extension of that love. Sex is a normal part of adult relationships. The more comfortable you are with sex and your body, the better the experience of love-making will be.

It's also an important interplay between masculine and feminine energy. If you are in a relationship and you are not having sex, you won't feel as sexual or sensual. You will start to feel less feminine. The same goes for a man – if a masculine man is in a relationship and he is capable of having sex and he's not, he will feel less desired, less loved and he could feel less masculine.

To make him feel more masculine, remember that masculine energy loves to control, including in the bedroom. Even though he still wants you to say what you like or don't like, or ask for certain things, he still likes to control and please.

If a feminine woman is trying to stay in control, on the other hand, she will find it hard to orgasm. In order to have an explosive orgasm, she has to feel totally out of control. She needs to open herself up to love and passion. She has to allow the pleasure to escape out of her. Something that makes sex exciting for the feminine is when she doesn't know what her partner is going to do next. That's where the passion and excitement starts.

A man also has to see that she's enjoying it in order to know that he's doing well. He will love it when his woman is free to be herself, when she surrenders and trusts in him. This forms an incredible bond and connection. It's an unbelievable feeling for someone to love you for you. It's an amazing feeling to be open and to relax into yourself while making love.

~ What masculine men say ~

Jerry, a masculine man from California, said it's all summed up in Usher's song: men want a lady on the street but a freak in the bed. Men love the light side, but also the dark side of a woman.

Sometimes the spark won't come back

No matter how hard you try, sometimes nothing will entice you back to wanting to have sex with someone. Sometimes you just lose those feelings. Sometimes reality hits and it's clear that, while you love the person, you just don't want to be intimate with them.

Banish The Bitch And Bring Out The Babe

Brett and Jenny were together for over ten years. They loved each other without question. They lived together and they looked after each other. Yet they had not been intimate for many years. Jenny said that Brett became like her best friend or her brother… she could not think of him as her lover anymore.

They separated and within three months Jenny met someone else. Brad swept her off her feet. Something in her stirred that she had not felt for a long time. She found a burning desire to be intimate with this new man she had met. She felt a spark; she felt a real attraction.

She said that, in her opinion, in a normal, healthy relationship, wanting to be intimate with someone (or not) could very well be the difference between 'loving' someone and being 'in love' with someone. She said that she had loved Brett deeply but was not 'in love' with him.

> *Husbands are like fires. They go out when unattended.*
>
> – Zsa Zsa Gabor

(The same can be said for wives)

Exercise

1. If you are in a relationship and, for whatever reason, you are uncomfortable having sex with your partner, try and open yourself up to enjoyment. Even if it doesn't result in sex, try and relax a little more around them. Try and enjoy the connection you have with your partner. Look into their eyes, connect with them and try to feel what they are feeling.

Values

Every single person has different rules they live by. These rules originate from our individual values, which could have originated from our parents, school teachers, relatives, friends or any of our life's experiences. If two people have conflicting values, they will struggle to create a harmonious relationship together.

Our values guide our everyday actions. They define what we believe is right or wrong and good or bad. They are our rules for moral conduct and define our personal standards.

These values are incredibly important, as they will determine our life's path. They can also help us to balance our masculine and feminine energy, as well as to choose the right partner.

I believe these values live in our heart, and although we can try to rationalise decisions or actions that are contrary to our values, this will always create inner conflict. Think about a time when you did something that you thought wasn't the right thing to do and yet you did it anyway. Your heart was saying no while your head commanded you to do it anyway.

That conflict comes with a price. When our heart is telling us not to do something and we go ahead and do it anyway, it's painful. For example, if one of our rules is that we would never have a 'one-night stand' and we do, that will create inner conflict where we might be questioning our actions, beating ourselves up or feeling guilty.

If you are always upset or feeling out of sorts, look to see if you are living against your values. The goal is for your life to align with your values – personally, professionally and with your partner – in order to live in congruency.

As far as relationships are concerned, conflicts in values could be a major issue. If one of your main values in life is to help animals and you work for a wildlife protection association, yet your partner loves hunting, things will be strained to say the least. Likewise, if your highest values in life are security and certainty and your partner's highest value is living on the edge in all aspects, you will struggle to find a balance that keeps you both happy.

On the other hand, if you share your most important values, your relationship will complement and supplement the rest of your life. You will likely have similar interests, you will enjoy doing the same things, and you will also be comfortable giving each other the space to do the things you love to do independently. Work, love and life will no longer feel so hard. Making each other feel loved won't feel so hard. You won't feel like you're alone. You will be able to share your experiences with someone else on your level. That's when you can experience inner peace.

What do you both value in your relationship?

Consider what you value in your relationship. Some common values include:

1. Staying true to yourself – You are your own person and you don't want to change who you are.
2. Love and connection – You give love to and feel love from your partner.
3. Attraction/chemistry – You have an attraction or spark.
4. Alignment – You are both on the same wavelength.
5. Mutual respect – You would never disrespect the other person.
6. Polarity – There is masculine and feminine energy in your relationship.
7. Honesty – You are truthful and loyal to each other.
8. Great sex – You are open and free to be intimate with your partner.
9. Laughter and fun – You can make each other laugh and have fun.
10. Excitement – You have a passion for life.

Chapter 7: Your relationship foundations – How to keep your soul mate

Get an understanding of your own values. Then, once you have been through this exercise, ask your partner to select his top relationship values. Are they similar?

If they are not similar to yours, this may help you to highlight why you are not seeing eye to eye in some areas. For instance, if your top values are love and connection and mutual respect, yet your partner's values are great sex and excitement, you might have slightly different thoughts about where you are going to participate in love-making.

Mr Big had many masculine values at the top of his list: success, significance, wealth, status, abundance and more. However, none of his values related to personal fulfilment – they were all work-related. Love, health, happiness, fun, spirituality and adventure didn't appear on his list.

He drove himself nearly into the ground to achieve his goals. Later in life, his heart began to tell him to focus on love and he pushed those feelings aside.

Over time, he slowly began to acknowledge that there was more to life than work. After a few years, he said he began to adjust his values to begin to allow love to become a priority. He said he recognised that he had to open up his heart and his life to feel love. Doing this also made way for deeper relationships with his family and friends. He had to adjust his beliefs and ingrained values relating to success and work to allow him to feel these feelings.

When you have different values…

I can't suggest how to prioritise your values. No one can. It's a very personal decision and one that is different for everyone. There is no wrong or right way to set your values – you need to see what works for you. You just need to make sure that your values don't conflict with your beliefs and preferably also align with your partner's beliefs. Keep in mind that, if your values are the complete opposite of your man's, you may begin to live very different lives.

Twenty years ago, I had success, wealth, achievement and similar values at the top of my list. It made me focus on work as my main priority. I did not focus on love or relationships. After realising my life was all about work, I saw that I needed to move love and connection, friends and relationships up towards the top of my list. Just that shift alone allowed me to create a more balanced life.

Today, my top three values are health, success, and love and connection. Prioritising your values is a very powerful thing to do. By changing your values, you change your life. You need to work out what you value most and how you want your life to be. Know that you may need to adjust them as time goes on.

After doing the previous exercise, you might discover that your and your partner's values are not the same.

This isn't always a bad thing. After all, we're all different. Some people are driven by success and they are willing to sacrifice love or relationships to achieve their success. Others like to focus on their children and the family unit first. We need values that will align and work in harmony.

There are two things to consider if you have different values.

First, do you contradict each other?

If you value certainty and you want to be at home every day but your partner wants to jump out of perfectly good planes, it may cause problems. If you want to save for a house but he likes to gamble and risk your life savings, there might be issues. If you value health and you exercise religiously and you eat healthy while he smokes and drinks, you might find it hard. You may end up with issues between you.

Second, do you have a mutual agreement that a foundation of love, support and understanding is important? This is the basis for your relationship. Do you also have some common goals beneath those values?

Are you 'in love?' Do you want to be with this person for the rest of your life? Can you see yourself being with them? Are you really good together? Do you really love each other?

Chapter 7: Your relationship foundations – How to keep your soul mate

When values become rules

Rules go hand in hand with values, as we have certain rules that need to be met in order to feel like we're living our values.

For instance, I remember attending a five-day Anthony Robbins event in Fiji where there were only fifty people in attendance. He had participants complete a process whereby each person had to write down their top values and their rules for what had to happen in order for them to feel like they had achieved those values or feelings.

My top five values were:

- Success
- Significance
- Wealth
- Recognition
- Achievement

Now, looking back, I can see that I definitely had very focused and directed values. No wonder I felt so masculine at the time!

Completing this process can be surprising. I was astonished at what I had written – love was not even on my list. And my rules for what I had to achieve before I could even feel successful, happy, healthy, loved or any of it would be absolutely impossible to reach.

As an example, in order to feel 'Successful', the rules that I had set for myself were that I had to have the biggest business of its kind in the area, *and* I had to have the largest number of staff turning over the highest amount of sales, *and* I had to make an astronomical amount of money every year, *and* I had to have everyone's respect, *and* I had to win every award there was in my field... The list went on and on and on. Interestingly, a lot of my goals were reliant on other people as I had to have staff doing unbelievable things as well. I was constantly relying on other people and their actions before I could even let myself think about being happy. I was never, ever, ever going to be truly happy as long as I kept those rules.

Most disagreements in relationships can be traced back to your rules and values. If you're upset, it's because your partner is not abiding by the rules you have set. The thing to keep in mind is that most of these rules are unspoken, so while you have things that you expect and would like him to do, he probably doesn't even know what your rules and expectations are.

For instance, if you think a guy should ask you to meet his parents after the third date, otherwise he can't love you, how is he supposed to know that is one of your rules? Meanwhile, the guy might have his own rule that says he doesn't introduce a girl to his parents until he knows for sure that she's a 'keeper'.

The biggest point I want you to gain out of this is that you may need to relax your rules. You need to realise that your rules are your rules. The more rules you have, the more unhappy you will be. I don't care how right you think your rules are, they might not be for everyone. Remember that every time you're upset, it's you feeling like someone has broken your rules.

Jenny was dating John for about three months. The morning of her birthday, she hoped he would take her to breakfast; that was her ideal way to start the day. John was busy with his friends that morning and he called to tell her he would take her for lunch instead. She was really angry that he didn't take her to breakfast. He was in shock as he didn't see the difference between breakfast and lunch. She caused a major fight between them on her birthday. All because he didn't know her rules. If you are like Jenny and this happens to you, ask yourself, would they have even known your rules? You might need to assess your behaviour and, at the same time, lighten up.

I used to be fanatical about cleaning the house. I loved to have everything in its place. I loved the house tidy but it also stressed me out. Especially when children came along. I decided that I wanted to be happy, not stressed. I decided that I wouldn't get so upset about the house being as tidy. This is how I relaxed some rules. For example,

Chapter 7: Your relationship foundations – How to keep your soul mate

when I got the urge to get up and put the toys away – I made myself sit down. I made myself remember that they would only turn up on the lounge room floor again tomorrow. When I got the urge to mop the floor for the third time in the week, I relaxed my rules. I set it that I would do the floors once a week.

When you are upset, really analyse your rules. Analyse your upsets. What was it exactly that made you unhappy? What did you expect to happen? Were you upset at your partner? Why were you upset? Did your partner even know that you got upset or why you got upset? Talk about your rules, if you have to, with your partner. Likewise if they are upset with you, what are their rules? What did they expect from you?

If you both don't know what your rules are, you can't help each other. The point I am making here is that you might have to really work on relaxing what you think everyone else should do. Or you may need to come to a compromise. For your own peace of mind.

If you believe your rules are unbreakable, you may need to communicate these to your partner so they know.

Common goals

What's the purpose of being in a relationship? It's important for both partners in a relationship to agree on a purpose. By having a shared purpose, you will create opportunities to grow together, help each other remain true to yourselves and help one another achieve the highest potential. For both partners to be happy, that's the ultimate relationship.

Common goals help keep the passion and excitement alive. When you have something to work towards with common interests, it's then you have a true purpose for being together. Even if that purpose is to make each other happy.

As I've discussed, the masculine generally finds it easier to focus on his work than his relationship, as he feels he has more control over his work than his partner. He is also rewarded for this focus as it's easier for him to see measurable results at work.

However, if the feminine feels like she and their children should be a higher priority, this can easily lead to conflict.

Instead, imagine if both partners committed to the common goal of caring for your family. If he values work and material success highly, the goal behind his work might be providing for your family. He can then focus on work and she can feel good about it, knowing that he's doing it for her and their children. Meanwhile, the way she contributes to this common goal is by focusing on her partner and their children.

To keep your relationship passionate and to make your relationship measurable, it is beneficial to have joint goals that you both can look forward to and work towards.

Create common goals

When you are in a committed relationship, think about the goal you could have with your partner. No matter how big or small, it's something you could do together.

Discuss what you and your partner would love to do or achieve together. What's something you can both look forward to? Do you want to buy a house, go on a holiday, or make plans for when you retire? Do you want to support a charity together? What do you both love to do? What can you both do together?

Discuss what your goals could be and write them somewhere where you will see them regularly.

The more you clarify and discuss these with your partner, the more your relationship will develop. At least once a month, take the time to plan some exciting goals together. Get excited and talk about how you can support and encourage each other.

Chapter 7: Your relationship foundations – How to keep your soul mate

The three grand essentials of happiness are: something to do, someone to love, and something to hope for.

– Alexander Chalmers

Summary

If only I knew then what I know now…

- Always remember to be conscious of the polarity in your relationship. Remember the rules of engagement we discussed earlier.
- To have the best relationship possible, the two people involved must trust each other enough to communicate. It's only through deep communication that they will truly feel deeper love.
- We all feel love in different ways. Recognise that how you will feel loved is different to how your partner or even your children will feel loved.
- It will help you enormously to consider if a potential partner has similar values to you. Understand that everyone has different rules and expectations; once you accept this, it can help you relate to others more, and also be more empathetic towards them.

Exercises

1. What are the five top feelings you care about more than anything else in the world? Really think about how these things are affecting your life. What are you missing out on because you have these five things at the top of your list?

2. What do you really want to keep up the top of your list that is serving you?

3. What's a rule you have that causes you a lot of stress? For example, do you have a rule that your partner needs to put his plate in the dishwasher, or he needs to put the toilet seat down? What would it mean to you if you were to let go of the stress associated with that situation?

Chapter 8: If things go wrong

Our relationships can turn sour for many reasons. Some of these reasons are:

- We chose the wrong partner in the first place.
- One partner grows in a different direction to the other, or both mature differently. If our values, rules and goals change and we are no longer aligned.
- We never had polarity or we lose polarity.
- Both parties in the relationship don't feel loved – we don't understand each other's love language.
- We fall out of love with our partner and intimacy stops.
- Our lifestyle choices change.
- We try and make a man our project and we then realise they are not going to change.
- Interdependent relationships.
- Affairs.

Interdependent relationships

Interdependency is when two people in a relationship have blended into one. They rely on each other for love and connection. They rely on each other to feel certain and to feel strong. They look to each other for significance, variety, growth and spirituality.

Ultimately, they feel like they need each other to survive.

The end result, though, is that they don't have the same zest for life. They feel incredibly unhappy in their relationship and they don't know why.

They feel like they've lost their individual identities.

The truth is, they feel trapped.

Maryanne and John had a business together that employed fifteen staff members. They both had clear roles in the business: Maryanne did the accounting and bookwork and John ran the staff and the operations of the business.

Maryanne and John also had four children and a large family. It took a lot of hard work to keep their family together. Maryanne and John could not see how they could run their lives without each other. They felt trapped both by their business responsibilities and their family responsibilities. They just weren't happy together. Feeling trapped made it so much worse.

Types of interdependent relationships

Several things can happen where partners in a relationship believe that they need each other to survive.

- One of the partners could become a dominator. They could use emotional or financial blackmail to make their partner feel like they have to stay in the relationship.
- One of them could put themselves in the position of becoming a victim, making the other person feel responsible for them.

- They could both feel trapped financially. They could feel like they would suffer greatly financially by separating or they could believe that they couldn't survive financially without the other.
- Their self-confidence could be so low that they feel they could never attract anyone else. They could feel stuck with who they are with.

Leaving interdependent relationships

While those in interdependent relationships often don't particularly want to be in the relationship, a lot of them don't leave. Just some of the reasons why they stay include:

- They have relied on their spouse for so many things over the years and their spouse fills a great part of their needs. Even though they are incredibly unhappy, they see more pain associated with leaving than they do with staying. It all seems too hard to leave.
- They stay together because of the drama. If one partner finally decides that they will end the relationship, the other can pull every trick out of the book to try and get them to stay. Sometimes, they end up staying as the only way they know how to handle the drama is to stay. For example, if the man in the relationship has an alcoholic wife, he may try and leave the relationship. He might not know how to cope with her alcoholism, especially if there are children involved. She may get drunk and cause significant problems, so much so that he can't see a way of leaving. He may choose to stay and try to handle the drama instead.
- Some people stay because they rationalise that they are sacrificing their happiness for the benefit of the rest of the family.

Banish The Bitch And Bring Out The Babe

In the end, putting all stories and excuses aside, they more than likely just don't have the confidence and courage to leave.

Sometimes it is hard to see the forest for the trees. When you are in a dysfunctional relationship, it can become somewhat normal to you no matter how mucked up it is to others. But it could be all you've ever known. If this is you, try and have a break from the relationship for a few months. Try and get some space to think about what you really want in life. Get your mind clear.

Affairs – just don't do it!

June and Michael had been married for ten years and they hadn't had sex for over four years. While they both talked about the situation, nothing changed. June ended up having an affair as a result.

She didn't tell Michael, and it soon affected her immensely. Affairs went against everything she had ever believed and it conflicted strongly with her values of honesty, love, caring and loyalty. Before long, she couldn't even look Michael in the face because of the guilt she felt. These feelings were soon negatively anchored to Michael, so that anytime she looked at him she felt all those feelings of guilt, anger and sadness, even though it wasn't his fault.

They separated about two years later. June never told him what had happened. She never recovered from the guilt she felt.

Affairs hurt everyone.
Very rarely do they have a happy ending.

What do I mean by an affair? An affair is premeditated adultery.

I believe that an infidelity is an infidelity – no matter how small, it's a betrayal. However, the level at which it is seen as wrong is up to the individual. My belief is if you have emotional ties to someone apart from your partner, even the 'little things' also count as betrayal. If you feel you need to lie, then there is a good chance it's a betrayal. Some

Chapter 8: If things go wrong

people believe a one-night stand should be seen as a mistake, an accident or something that should never have happened. Some think it's okay to move on as if it didn't happen. Some people say that if it meant nothing to them, they would never risk telling their partners and risk losing everything.

An affair is when this infidelity continues. It is a conscious decision to follow what might have been a one-off with ongoing adultery. Maybe it wasn't premeditated the first time you got together… but every time after, it is.

Regardless of your role in the affair, affairs rarely end well. The guilt involved can be huge. Once the person who has been cheated on discovers the infidelity, they can get upset and angry. When children are involved, whole worlds could be turned upside down with serious emotional and financial ramifications.

If you are thinking about having an affair, consider a few things before you do. How do you think your property settlement will be effected? How do you think your financial situation will unfold? How do you think your relationship with your partner and your relationship with your children will be affected? What will happen if your friends and family find out?

The cost of an affair is very steep.

My advice is not to have any indiscretions.

For the one being cheated on, it's devastating to their self-esteem. If they feel like they don't have other options, they can feel powerless and desperate, and they may do everything to keep their partner. They will feel unwanted, unloved and feel like they weren't enough for their partner.

For the other woman, it's extremely hard knowing the person she loves is with someone else. Someone they have ties with; someone they have a history with. Someone who potentially knows them better than she does. Someone who knows how to push their buttons, if they need to.

And for the cheater, even though it can be exhilarating at first, the more they have to lie and hide and skulk around without getting caught, the more difficult the affair becomes to sustain, especially when their partner at home starts getting suspicious or the other person becomes demanding.

Simply do not get involved in affairs at any stage or at any time. Affairs are wrong. They hurt people. They can be soul-destroying for all those affected.

Why would someone have an affair?

People who have affairs usually have a void in their existing relationship or in their life in general. If needs are not being met in a relationship, they look to fill those needs elsewhere.

Some people will try to get their needs met by focusing on their work. This will be okay for a while, as the initial rush of new achievements fulfils them. However, before long, they'll start to reflect… 'Work's great, the kids are great, I have money, I have everything I could want. Why aren't I happy?'

If they're not feeling loved, temptation can strike when they least expect it. They might attract attention from someone new, or they might notice that they feel attracted to someone else.

It often starts as something innocent – catching up as friends for coffee or lunch. And they start to think, 'Wow! That person thinks I'm good-looking/nice/smart.' If they haven't had that kind of attention in a long time, it can feel amazing. Before long, it can unleash a spark they haven't felt for a long time.

They feel a connection. They feel significant. They feel loved. They experience variety. Their unmet needs get met almost instantly. They know it's wrong, but they suddenly feel alive. They feel a love and a lust they haven't experienced in years. Between the two relationships, they also feel complete. This is why affairs can feel addictive.

Chapter 8: If things go wrong

Not everyone will cheat. Keeping in mind that some couples have agreements that make it perfectly okay for them to have sex with others, many have to justify it somehow, usually in one of the following ways:

- They say that the affair didn't mean anything – it just happened, like it was an accident. (I've never seen a penis accidentally fall into a vagina, so I'm not sure how that works...)
- They say that they really love the other person, and they are torn between love and responsibility.
- They say it's only short-term – it's not going to go anywhere.
- They say it's only a long-distance relationship. They believe that because it's overseas, no real damage can be done, right?
- They feel complete with both relationships supplementing each other.
- They want to keep their options open.
- They have a higher libido than their partner.
- They want to feel loved.
- They don't want to hurt anyone by ending either relationship.

When someone knowingly becomes the 'other woman', she can get brought into it in a number of ways:

- She believes the person she is seeing will leave their partner and commit to a relationship with her. He's told her in no uncertain terms he will leave his wife.
- She has just come out of a long-term relationship and the arrangement suits her. She doesn't want or need anything of a permanent nature anyway.
- She might see it as a challenge or a test to see how much he loves her. ('If he really loves me, he'll leave his wife.')

Because affairs can fill a void, they can be addictive. Any relationship can be addictive when the other person meets your needs.

~ What masculine men say ~

Paul from Port Macquarie said that he has been married for over seven years to his wife. He would not even think of cheating on her as their values are aligned and his family unit is very important to him. However, he did cheat in previous relationships. The relationships where he cheated, he had never committed fully. He now has children and that changed the way he looked at fidelity. Commitment is extremely important to him.

When you are the one who's being cheated on

It's gut-wrenching. You feel betrayed. You don't feel safe; your certainty has been knocked out of you. You feel extremely vulnerable.

All of a sudden you feel like you don't know the person you are with. You feel like you are in a relationship with a stranger. You made commitments to each other to be together and you may have children. You thought you were going to be together forever. You thought they were loyal. You thought that you could trust them.

Your world as you know it has been turned upside down. You feel alone as your partner is no longer on your side. Now it feels like he's on an opposing team. You're no longer a couple as you know it – there's now a third person in the mix.

How could they do it? How could they betray your trust? How could they have sex with someone and come home to you and look you in the eye and lie? How could they swear they were telling you the truth? How could they act like nothing happened? How could they affect your family unit like this? How could they destroy your family?

You will have a million questions *exploding* out of your head.

You will feel anger, grief and incredible hurt. It's like your best friend has stuck a knife in your back and then twisted it. You will feel stupid as you think, 'How could I not have known it was happening?'

You will want to know who the other woman is and what she has that you don't. You will hate her. You will blame her. You will wonder what made him attracted to her and not you. You will doubt yourself.

It's easy to blame the other woman. It's easy to say it was her fault.

You know, though, if it didn't happen with her, it probably would have happened with someone else. It very well could have happened with others; it's not their fault. It was most likely a fault in your relationship, a void or a need that wasn't being met. You can blame the other person, however, you also have to look at how you and your partner showed up in your relationship. Do you also need to take some responsibility or blame? Did you recognise there was a problem yet you ignored it? If you chose to ignore the problems, you chose to neglect your relationship.

Moving forward, what can you do? You have three choices:

- You allow them to keep having the affair.
- You end your relationship.
- You give them an ultimatum – 'It's her or me.' If he chooses you, you then do everything you can to work out your problems and move on.

When it comes to making your decision, keep your self-esteem in check. Don't settle for someone who cheated on you because you feel you don't have other options. Only choose to stay if you really believe you can be happy in the relationship again.

Remember, you deserve to have it all.

When you are the other woman

When you begin, it could start with lunch, dinner or a coffee. It's not an affair. It's just two friends going out together. He may start to flirt with you a little to test your receptiveness to his advances. He might casually fill you in about the problems he's having with his wife. He'll probably tell you that he's going to leave her.

If there's an attraction and a spark, that's when things start to turn dangerous. It's about now that you assure yourself that your friendship won't lead to anything. If it does, he said he's leaving his wife anyway. It can't hurt... Besides, it's not your fault. One thing leads to another and before you know it, you are entangled in a messy love affair.

Time passes and you fall deeply in love. But, despite what he has told you, he's still with his wife. To cope, you decide to take it day by day. You might try to put his wife out of your mind... but it starts eating away at you. You wonder what's really happening between them.

You could leave him, but you are in love. Plus, from how bad he *says* he has it at home, you still think he will leave. He insists he's going to leave. You even feel sorry for him, as he says he has it so bad. He might say that he's upset or sick. (Note: this could be his way to try to get your sympathy while he is most likely with his wife.)

You tell yourself it's going to be okay, and you honestly think it's going to be okay. Your relationship will be different to all the other affair disasters that you've heard about. After all, *your* man loves you.

Statistics say that only five percent of married men ever leave their wives. Prepare yourself; there is a great chance he won't ever leave. If he had the courage to leave, he would have done so before he got involved with you.

Life in an affair is a sickening roller coaster. One minute you are high on love, then you are in the pits of hell. The relationship starts with promises – when you are single and you begin an affair with someone married, they can promise you all kinds of things. Usually, they tell you that they will leave their partner and you believe them. You *want*

Chapter 8: If things go wrong

to believe them. You *want* to trust them. Once you have fallen in love with them, you hope, you wish and you want to believe.

The reality is that, instead of building a relationship on love, maturity and trust, the relationship is built on a foundation of dishonesty. While those who instigate affairs sometimes have good intentions of leaving their partner, others have no intention of leaving at all. If they were really considering leaving their partner, they would already be taking action.

The reality is that you don't see what's happening at home. They will tell you they are not intimate with their spouse, but you will never know. You will then have to live with your imagination. In most cases, they are lying to their partner *and* they are lying to you. Many are master manipulators, who manipulate each person and the situation so they can have their cake and eat it too. Don't think for a minute that they are being honest with you.

As the other woman, even when you're single, you will also get dragged into the deception. You will still have to lie and hide. You'll constantly feel like you're doing the wrong thing. You'll also feel like you have to protect them. You have to be careful what you say, what you do and who sees you. You could be constantly living in a state of paranoia.

When you're single, in times of trouble, they can feel like your certainty and your rock. However, they can also make you want to cry yourself to sleep on lonely nights.

Don't mistake an affair for a real relationship. They're not your other half – they are your 1/10th (if you are lucky). You are their mistress, and that's all. You will only get crumbs of their time, even though it can feel special because they made time just for you. Being the 'other woman', when things get tough, you will always be his lowest priority. You are the lowest hanging fruit. You're the easiest one to get rid of. Your situation is the least complicated to deal with. They will not make you a priority as long as they have their partner at home.

They are not your partner – they are just a character in the little bubble of your affair. You don't see them in normal life – you don't see them with their friends and family, you don't get to experience the highs and lows of life together, you don't get to experience special occasions and more. They are with their wife and family.

Your affair is not real life. It's make-believe. It's fantasy. This makes it impossible to gauge how they would show up in a normal relationship.

Before you get in too deep, if you really love the person and you would like to have a relationship with them, tell them to come back once they have separated. Tell them to go away and work out what they want to do.

Yes, it's hard! The feelings they give you can be addictive. They fill or at least supplement your needs.

You need to remember that *you* are in control of you. You can change the situation at any time. If you find yourself in this situation, the smart thing would be to break it off. If you feel like you can't break it off, at least start dating other people. Do not close yourself off to opportunities. You'll never really know if they have plans to leave their partner, and you don't want to wake up in five years still being the other woman.

Don't live in the state of hope.
Live in reality and have hope.

When you are the cheater

You've been in a loveless marriage for some time. Then, one day you find someone who generates a spark in your world. Someone who pays you some attention, attention like you haven't felt in a long time. You feel ecstatic, like you're on a high. Before long, you feel like you have finally found love again.

You have stability at home and variety and excitement with this new person. You suddenly feel alive. You feel special, you feel needed and you feel loved.

You have to juggle a lot of balls, though. You have to lie to both of the men in your life. Then you have to remember your lies. You also have to cover up your lies. You have to try to keep two people happy. It's extremely tiring. You have great days with one, then down days with the other, and if they both have problems then you have to try to make out you're interested.

If you have children, this adds another level of complexity. You have responsibilities to your children and your current partner. There is the potential for huge financial ramifications. And then there's the guilt.

You might be trying to work towards an exit strategy, or you might prefer not to think about it – it all seems too hard. You might rather bury your head in the sand, have an affair and hope you can have the best of both worlds.

When you have an affair, you are getting your desire for love from an intimate partner filled by two people. Your existing partner may contribute certainty, security and stability. However, if you're looking elsewhere (or are tempted to look elsewhere) to have needs like excitement and variety met, this means there are many other gaps in this love. If you desire an affair, your real desire is to fill your desire for love from your intimate partner, and you feel you need to supplement your partner to do that. Bringing in a lover helps fill those gaps, which can give you a sense of feeling complete.

Ultimately, your needs are being met by two people. Your need for certainty is met by your partner at home, while your need for excitement, adventure and variety is met by your affair. When it goes well, a lot of people don't want to change that. You feel happy and have a sense of peace. You might think it's easier to be involved with two people than to find one person who can fill both roles.

You might even justify your reasons for being in an affair – you might say it's for your children or for work. In reality, the only one benefitting from this situation is you, and usually that's only when it goes well.

Banish The Bitch And Bring Out The Babe

Before long, it becomes a challenge to keep all of those balls in the air. So many things can go wrong. You can get caught out on your lies. Your partner could give you an ultimatum or the one you are having the affair with could give you an ultimatum. What happens if your kids, family and friends find out? This does not only affect you; it affects the whole family. It affects everything.

Summary

If only I knew then what I know now…

- Never ever enter into an affair. Ever. Only ever consider a relationship if the man is available. It doesn't matter what he says. It's what he does that counts.

Exercises

1. If you have been involved in any part of an affair, how did you feel? What did you learn from it?
2. Do you know anyone else that has been involved in an affair? What did you learn?

Chapter 9: Relationship breakdowns

Forty to forty-five percent of first marriages end in divorce. The statistics go up to sixty to sixty-seven percent for second marriages and seventy to seventy-three percent for third marriages.

Why are the statistics so high? On analysing separations, there are a number of different scenarios.

The first scenario is we simply grow apart. When a couple first start to date, they have become who they are as a result of their experiences so far in life. When you're in a relationship, there could be times when you both grow together and there could be times where you both grow separately. There are also times where you simply grow in two separate directions, and you may realise that you are no longer suited to each other.

Some people can blame a mid-life crisis on a failed relationship. I don't see this as a case of someone trying to reclaim their youth, but of someone taking a good look at their life and realising that they are not where they want to be. Different things can trigger the 'crisis' – a birthday ending in zero, a death in the family, being fed-up in a job, or not experiencing real love in their relationship (or anywhere else, for that matter).

They realise that they need to change something. If they don't, they know that they will stay where they are for the rest of their lives. Both scenarios can scare them to death. The thought of staying where they are living the same life they are living, especially if they are miserable, can be unbearable. When it comes to the feminine and masculine, each may be looking for something different in this change.

The feminine will generally have wanted to end a relationship because her need for love and connection wasn't being met at the level she needed. Maybe she didn't feel safe or she didn't feel protected or her rules for love were not being met. If her man was a 'pleaser', she could have felt like she became the man. She may have lost respect for him for not stepping into the masculine role.

The masculine, on the other hand, will consider breaking up with his partner if he thinks the feminine is holding him back from his goals, if he doesn't feel loved by her at the deepest level, if he thinks she doesn't respect him, or if he believes that he's done his best and he can't make her happy.

In any of these situations, one of them may leave the relationship or they may just supplement the relationship with something or someone else.

The fact is, if you're miserable in your relationship, you are miserable. And relationship problems soon transfer to every other area of your life. If you want to create an amazing life, your relationships need to be a priority.

The 4Rs of deterioration

Deteriorating relationships go through many stages. In Barbara De Angeles's *How to Make Love All the Time*, she calls these the 4Rs, or Resistance, Resentment, Rejection and Repression.

Chapter 9: Relationship breakdowns

This is my interpretation of them:

- **Resistance** is where you have little pet hates about one another. It might be that someone leaves the toilet seat up, they didn't get you flowers on Valentine's Day or they didn't support you in an issue that you felt was important. It can be lots of tiny little things that annoy the heck out of you. While these things don't seem to be much of a problem, they really, *really* annoy you and each time your partner does one of them, you feel more and more angry. This can lead to resentment.

- **Resentment** develops after feeing upset over a prolonged period. You could unconsciously stack those feelings on top of each other until they form negative anchors. Your partner may do one little thing and then everything they have ever done that annoyed you comes flooding back. In this stage, you get upset and angry easily. You still love them, but things they do just seem to annoy you more and more, to the point of making you angry. Soon you don't feel as loving towards them as you used to. You need to address this level, as it will lead to rejection.

- **Rejection** involves rejecting the person. You reject their opinion, their sexual advances and their love. At this stage, you're on the way out – mentally and possibly physically.

- **Repression** is when you just don't care anymore. You are over fighting it or feeling anything about it. You have no emotion. You are not interested in fixing the relationship because you've detached yourself so much from the other person. At this time, the other party might be looking for an easy fix. He might want to go to counselling, but at this point you've simply had enough and you don't want to fix it.

As you can see, each of these stages adds another nail to the relationship's coffin.

~ What masculine men say ~

Jerry from San Diego travelled a lot for work. He used to love getting on a plane and leaving his partner at home. He knew that he was much happier when he was away from his wife than when they were together. He also said when he looked back on photos with his wife, he was never smiling. The minute he left, he said he felt liberated and free. He was so much happier away from their toxic relationship.

The options

What do you do if both parties are extremely unhappy in the relationship?

That's for each person to decide. The options are:

- You can do everything you can think of to make it work.
- You can emotionally leave the relationship and distract yourself by throwing yourself into something else, like work.
- You can physically leave the relationship.

How can you 'fix' your relationship?

I find that, in most breakups, both parties did not do everything they could to save the relationship. While they might say they did, when it comes down to it, they didn't.

If your relationship is suffering and you are doing exactly the same thing – *stop!* You must do something different to realise a different result.

Here are some things you can do that might help:

- Tell your partner exactly how you feel.
- Go to counselling together.

Chapter 9: Relationship breakdowns

- Read some books together on relationships.
- Listen to some audios together on relationships.
- Talk to your partner about ways you can make your relationship better.
- Engage a life coach or a relationship coach.
- Go to some good quality relationship workshops.
- Move away from each other for a couple of months to clear your heads.

Once you've done those things, you can determine where you want to be in your relationship.

Niki was working full-time and had become the bread-winner and the masculine energy in her relationship with Tom. When Niki was six-months pregnant with their second child, she discovered that Tom had been cheating on her for some time.

While she didn't condone it, she felt like she was stuck in the relationship. She was scared as she had no idea how she would survive in the future if they weren't together.

Because of this, she became desperate to try and make him stay. She tried to entice him with more sex, hoping he then wouldn't need it from anywhere else. She did his washing, made his favourite meals, watched sports on TV and let him go wherever he wanted. She basically did whatever he wanted. Her self-esteem got lower and lower.

Meanwhile, in his affair, Tom felt great. He felt like a man again. He had someone who wanted him and who desired him, so he kept the affair going, despite Niki knowing.

This left Niki feeling like a doormat. She felt unwanted and unloved, and eventually she decided to move out.

After a period of time, Niki found a new boyfriend and commenced a committed relationship with him. Soon they moved in together.

Banish The Bitch And Bring Out The Babe

Once Tom saw this, he freaked out. He saw someone else raising his child, he saw someone else loving his partner, and he wanted her back. He asked her to talk and they talked for hours. They talked about where things went wrong. They talked about how they both felt. They realised that they still had an amazing connection and something to fight for – their children. Their children were worth the fight.

Even though the experience caused a lot of pain, now Tom and Niki are back together and say that something had to happen for their relationship to go to the next level.

Niki's grateful the affair happened. It made her strong, it made her set boundaries and she put herself first. Previously she would have put Tom and the kids first. However, this experience prompted her to reassess her needs and how they could fill each other's needs moving forward. She set new standards for herself and new standards for how she expected to be treated. Tom now knows what she will and won't stand for in their relationship. Now they're together on her terms.

Rather than trying to control him, as she had before in her masculine energy, she realised that she needed to do the opposite. She decided to be feminine, vulnerable and allow him to step up and be the man. He's now the provider and she's raising their three children.

The polarity in their relationship has been reinstated. They now have a much deeper relationship where communication is the key.

It takes two people to fix a relationship, but you need to be willing to fix it. If you're in the position where fixing what's wrong feels like too much work, then that's a red flag. While you might say you're willing to do anything, when it comes down to it, you're not. That's when you know it's over. When you don't want to try.

How to know if it's over

When I was deciding what to do about Mr Small, I did this exercise. I love this process as it's very visual and helps to get your thoughts clear.

Draw a line down the middle of a piece of paper. On one side, write the reasons why you *should* be with this person, and on the other, write the reasons why you *shouldn't* be with this person.

Which list is longer?

In my case, the list of reasons why I shouldn't have been with him far outweighed the other one. I realised I couldn't continue living that way. It was killing me.

Is it over?

If you're thinking about ending your relationship, ask yourself:

- Do you really love them?
- Are you 'in love' with them?
- Have you ever had a passionate relationship together?
- Is this relationship extremely important for you to save? Why/why not?
- What have you done to try and save the relationship?
- Will you do anything to save this relationship?
- What could you do to save the relationship?
- What advice would you give your best friend if they were in your situation?
- What wouldn't you do to try to save the relationship?
- What will you do now?

If it's over, why are you staying?

Obviously, not all relationships work. Yet many people choose to stay in dysfunctional relationships.

Some people don't want to be alone. After weighing up all the alternatives, they decide that it's easier to stay and settle.

Others don't want their lives to be turned upside down. Ending a serious relationship is disruptive, particularly if you are married or living together and have shared finances. If you have children, that makes things even more complicated. The dynamics of your family and circle of friends change with one less person, it can be financially devastating, and your work, friendships and security can suffer.

Some stay together for the children, either because they think their children will have a hard time dealing with the separation or because they came from a broken family and they don't want that for their children.

Some get the courage to leave and then they feel incredibly lonely and go back. They go back because it's what they know – the relationship is familiar. It also seems easier to stay than to start again with someone else.

Some stay because they associate more pain with leaving the relationship than they do with staying. It seems too hard.

Pride can also come into it – they don't want to let people think they failed at their marriage. This was a big one for me after I separated from Mr Beige. I felt like a failure. Now, I would consider it a failure if I stayed somewhere and I was miserable. I knew that it was going to be tough to walk from the relationship. There was always the risk of a bloody aftermath. I just couldn't bear the thought of staying with someone for the next twenty years if we weren't happy. I just couldn't. We had already stayed together for five years longer than we should have.

Some people stay because they don't want to hurt their partner. They love their partner, but they're not 'in love' with them. They think that if they stay, they can overlook what they see is not right about them.

They either think that they can live with their faults or they think they'll help their partner fix their faults.

Ultimately, these reasons can lead people to stay in loveless marriages for their whole adult lives without ever attempting to do anything to change them. Sometimes they simply don't know what to do.

The danger is that, if you stay in the relationship, you may be 'there but not there'. You may switch off emotionally from your partner and throw everything into work or your children. At least then you'll feel successful in one area of your life, right? The problem is that work can't fulfil all of your needs.

If you're considering staying for one of these reasons, it's important to consider the real reason you're staying. Is it really because of the kids? Is it because you're too scared to make the decision and take responsibility? Are you worried about finding someone new? What's the real reason? You need to get your heart out of the situation and think about what the best thing is for you, your partner and your children (if you have any).

Breaking up is hard to do!

When couples are having trouble in their relationships and they are thinking of calling it quits, some think that leaving is the easy way. Get this – it's not easy! You may have to go through the process of dividing your assets and, depending on your partner, this could be horrific. If you have children with this person, it could be a nightmare.

When I separated from Mr Beige, we had a business and lots of other ties together. For about two years, I felt trapped. I was scared, thinking that I couldn't leave the marriage even if I wanted too. Even though we didn't have children, we had employees, family and friends who would be affected by our separation.

Every single day I was very conscious that I didn't want to hurt him. Then I thought, 'Every day that we're in a marriage where we are anything but happy and fulfilled is hurting both of us.'

The other thing I considered was how having the business together affected things in our life. If we sold the business and we adjusted our lives accordingly, would we be happy together? The answer was no, we wouldn't. I looked at the end result and worked back. We needed to separate. Our end result, or what we needed to achieve, was to be friends no matter what. In that process, we did everything we could to be fair and understanding towards the other person. Knowing the outcome made it easier to plan and execute our separation.

We knew we both deserved more; we deserved to be happy. And it got to the stage where we knew that we were better to have one big hurt via a separation than to hurt every day. It was a big, tough decision.

It hurt both of us.

My belief is that if you have tried everything in your marriage and you're unhappy, then life is too short. Just because you married someone, it shouldn't mean you have to live unhappily as a sentence until death.

We are both so much happier now. Mr Beige is now married to a lovely girl and he's happy!

However, remember that every relationship is different and every situation is different. Each person has to work out what's right for their family. There are varying degrees of happiness and sadness. Some relationships have a chance of being fixed and some don't. Look to see where yours is on the scale.

It's not your responsibility to see how long you can last in a relationship. It's your job to act with integrity while in that relationship. Consult with your higher self and ask what the best thing is for you and your family. Sometimes the best thing to do is to stay. Only you can make that decision. You just need to decide.

If you do decide to stay, you must make the most of it and plan on making the most of your life. Make it the happiest that you can make it.

~ What masculine men say ~

Scott from Texas said to have the dignity and respect to tell your partner if you want to leave the relationship. If you know beyond any doubt that you don't want to be there any longer, act on it before it turns nasty and you come to resent each other. Scott regrets how he handled his separation. He said it didn't get quite as bad as the movie War of the Roses, but it got close. He now doesn't have the relationship with his ex-wife that he would have liked. It has hurt him a lot because his relationship with his children has also suffered.

When you are considering breaking up

When you consider ending a relationship, ask yourself this question: If you knew back then what you know now, would you still have moved forward with the relationship? If the answer is 'no', ask yourself another question: If you could click your fingers and there was no history, no past and no financial ties, would you leave the relationship? If the answer is 'yes', there's another big clue.

For the moment, just focus on whether or not you want to end it. Figuring out how to complete the process can come later. The most important thing initially is to get a 'yes' or 'no'. Stay or go? Then you can work out what to do from there.

A word of advice – if you *do* decide to break up, don't get out your old photos, don't watch your wedding DVD and don't look through keepsakes from your time together. Don't torture yourself. If you do this, you could end up remembering things being better than they were, and start longing to have things back the way you remember them.

Focus on analysing what happened. Better yet, get feedback from an outsider who knew you well and saw your relationship.

Banish The Bitch And Bring Out The Babe

After I split with Mr Small, I phoned a girlfriend who said, 'Great, you were never happy with him anyway.' At first this shocked me, but then I agreed. When I reflected, I hadn't been happy. I wasn't in love with him, but with what I hoped life with him would be. Hope was getting me by when, in fact, reality sucked. My girlfriend was right – I was a million times happier out of that relationship.

Make a decision, one way or the other

Sometimes we justify situations and we accept the way things are. Sometimes the situation is not ideal, but we can live with it, so we settle. It can seem less painful to stay the same rather than make a change.

That's okay, but you need to commit one way or the other. You are either staying or going – you can't be in your relationship with one foot out the door. If you commit to staying, you may need to burn your bridges behind you.

> *Having a 'yes' or a 'no', you can live with.*
>
> *'Maybes' make you miserable.*

Steve contacted me after his girlfriend broke it off with him. She had called the shots for most of the relationship. She held the power; she would tell them when they would see each other and what they would do.

He asked me how he could 'get over her'. I asked him to get out a piece of paper and to do the same exercise I recommended earlier – to draw a line down the middle and to write all the reasons why he should be with her on one side, and all the reasons why he shouldn't be with her on the other.

I asked him to then feel the emotion behind each of those reasons. I asked him to feel the pain of what it was like being in that relationship. I asked him to get angry and I asked him to get upset. I told him that

Chapter 9: Relationship breakdowns

he might not like her as much after this process as he needed to change the way he felt about her.

Because she had been in the masculine role in their relationship, I told him he needed to get his power back to stop the hurt he was feeling. He needed to get back control of his feelings. She was horrible to him and he needed to stop that. He needed to disassociate from her.

I knew from previous conversations that there were many more reasons to stay separated rather than to get back together – he just needed to commit to a clear 'yes' or 'no'. I explained that a 'yes' or a 'no' was easy to deal with. A 'yes' or a 'no' would allow him to make plans. He would know where he stood. Being the one to say 'yes' or 'no' would put him back in his power.

In relationships, the person with the power can offer plenty of 'maybes'. Offering 'maybes' allows them to dangle carrots of hope. But it leaves the other person vulnerable, uncertain and insecure.

We must always live in a state of reality, not in a state of hope. If you live in hope, you will be forever waiting and hoping for a different reality. On an ongoing basis, this becomes stressful. You don't want a 'maybe'.

In reality, you can only plan a future with who is with you *now*. If something happens later, you can adjust your plans. Don't put your life on hold for a maybe.

This is when you need to decide.

When you have definitive answers to situations, it's easy to plan. You can cut off all other options and focus fully in that direction. You can move forward with your life. You can make choices for the future.

Clarity and certainty equal emotional stability.
Emotional stability equals happiness and strength.

Banish The Bitch And Bring Out The Babe

How do you end it?

First, you need to make sure it's safe to end the relationship. If you think leaving your partner may put you or your children in danger, get help. Do you have to move out while he's not home? Do you need your family's support? Do you have to get help from the police or others? Assess your safety and do what works for you. Only you know your situation.

If you are safe to move forward, you could consider suggesting to your partner that you both take a break. Separate physically for a few months for a trial period and see how everything goes.

When you're away from the situation, you'll have time to get your head clear. You'll be able to see how you feel when you're not together. Separating in the short-term will let you see how you'll feel about it in the long-term. In some cases, you might realise that you do want to be with your partner after all, and you can recommit to saving the relationship.

In other cases, one or both of you may decide that the relationship is over.

When a relationship ends, most of the time, you'll experience heartbreak. It can take a while to move past the relationship, especially if your partner ended it. It could affect your self-confidence and could change your life dramatically, from your living situation and finances through to your social circle.

When your partner breaks up with you, you can feel like a lost puppy dog. You can feel betrayed and devastated. You can have all kinds of questions you want answered. Things you *need* answered.

You can feel that if they just answer your questions, you might be able to fix it, or at least understand it, and the pain will go away. You think that if you talk it through, you might be able to convince them otherwise.

If you are looking to get back together, ask yourself why you want to resurrect the relationship. What is the real reason?

- Is it because they fill a need in you, a void, something that's missing?
- Is it because you are scared to be alone?
- Do you really love them?
- Do you really want to be with them?

You can't control how another person thinks or feels. You can't control if they love you, you can't control if they lie to you and you can't control if they are cheating on you. You simply cannot control another person. You cannot control someone else's thoughts, actions or emotions.

When you separate, it can feel like you are a boat that has lost its anchor. It can feel like you are a piece of paper tumbling around in the wind, lost and out of control. It can feel like your certainty, your security and everything you know have dissipated. It can be incredibly scary. You can feel more alone than you have ever felt.

This is when you need to get back to basics. The focus needs to be on *you*. Build your foundations, release your negative beliefs, patterns and anchors, and reconnect to your feminine energy and your masculine energy. Build the foundations so that, if you run into a storm, you still feel safe and secure.

Life after breakup

Yes, there is a life after breakup.

When I was breaking up with Mr Small, I watched the movie *Sex and the City 2*. There was a scene in the movie where the girls were in Abu Dhabi. The girls were sitting in the desert and a guy came over the sand hills in a jeep. While watching that movie, I thought, 'Wow! I'm single – I could meet anyone in the world. How exciting!'

Banish The Bitch And Bring Out The Babe

After a breakup, you have options. You are free and independent once more. You could travel. You could learn a new skill. You could start a new career. When you're ready to meet someone new, you could meet anyone from anywhere. You could have a whole new adventure in life!

The danger is when you choose not to allow yourself to get hurt again. The problem with this is that you aren't allowing yourself to fall in love again, either. If you decide that you don't want to be open in your thoughts and feelings and you don't allow yourself to be vulnerable and open to love, you can erect massive protective barriers that don't let anyone in.

You have the power to allow yourself to be open, loving and vulnerable. It's the only way that you can ever experience real love. It also means that you are far more likely to get hurt. But, then again, if you don't experience love at the deepest level, that's going to hurt, too. Imagine never feeling true love, never feeling that special flutter in your tummy, and not feeling your heart skip a beat every time you see your true love.

Instead, why not give yourself the gift of being open, loving, vulnerable and feminine? You never know what (or who) might be around the next corner, so let yourself be open to the possibilities!

Summary

If only I knew then what I know now...

- 💚 If you find yourself in a relationship where you're very unhappy, analyse it. What's the problem? Did you choose the wrong person in the first place? Have you neglected each other over the years?

Chapter 9: Relationship breakdowns

- If your relationship isn't working, you have three options: You can explore every avenue to try to fix it, you can stay but try to get your needs met elsewhere, or you can leave.
- If you know you need to leave, then you need to leave. Breaking up with someone hurts, whether you're still in love with the person or not, and you may have countless reasons why you think you *should* stay, but if you're unhappy then you need to do what is right for you.
- The most important thing is to make a decision. You can live with a 'yes' or a 'no', but 'maybes' will make you miserable.

Exercises

The only exercise for this chapter is the following one.

If you are in a relationship and aren't sure whether you should still be together, grab a piece of paper. Draw a line down the middle.

On the top left-hand column, write: 'All the reasons I should be with [your partner]'. Then on the right-hand side, write: 'All the reasons I shouldn't be with [your partner]'.

See what comes out.

Chapter 10: Self-love, self-esteem and self-confidence

I used to walk into a room full of people and wonder if they liked me, now I look around and wonder if I like them.

— Unknown

Self-esteem, self-confidence and self-love are the references that you have about yourself. What you think of you. In the search to find your soul mate, there is no greater person to find than yourself.

These references can be different in each part of your life. You can have high opinions about yourself in some areas of your life and low opinions in other areas. For example, you could feel like you have your life sorted in your professional career, however, you are not confident with men. This is dangerous because, if you have made the love of an intimate partner an area where you don't feel confident, you may settle for less than you deserve.

Nothing is as important as your relationship with yourself.

Being able to love yourself keeps you healthy and happy and ensures you maintain your independence, even when you're in a relationship, rather than depending on your man to fill your needs for love.

Maintaining your own identity makes you strong and gives your life variety and colour, rather than making everything about him. Having your own identity helps you keep being the woman he fell in love with, while fulfilling your needs and building your confidence.

Finally, self-esteem gives you the freedom to make decisions that you're comfortable with, it gives you the confidence and the choice to speak up instead of following other people, and it gives you a voice.

There's nothing quite as sexy or beautiful as a woman who's confident in herself in a feminine way. A woman who's centred, strong, vulnerable and has a healthy dose of self-respect. When you have high self-love, your own identity and strong self-esteem, you have a certain aura or a presence about you. You hold your head up high and people are attracted to it. Men are attracted to it.

Today, I love myself and I'm going to act like it.

The four love buckets and how to fill them

Self-love is the most important thing you need to master in your life. After all, we all know that we can't rely on anyone else to make us happy except ourselves. The next section demonstrates why you shouldn't rely on external sources to feel love. The main reason being that you are not in control of other people and how they love you. You can only ever control your internal love. Self-love and self-acceptance are everything. As a feminine woman, love and connection are your greatest needs, and the first things you need to address.

There are four different types, or buckets, of love. They are:

Chapter 10: Self-love, self-esteem and self-confidence

- **Love of self** – You are totally responsible for the love felt in this category. This is the primary type of love and your foundation for stability as a human being. Self-love relates to your self-confidence and your self-worth. When you love yourself, you accept yourself unconditionally. This is the only bucket that you can control personally. It's the only love that comes from within. It's the only love that you can always rely on. This is the love that you need to focus on first. Your self-love must be constantly reinforced and guarded with your life.

- **Love from others** – This love relates to social acceptance and validation. The more self-love and self-confidence you have, the less social acceptance you will seek or need. This love can be filled by face-to-face interaction, text messages, phone calls and through interaction on social media. It's about relationships and networking. It can include both family and friends. It's a love without intimacy.

- **Love of an intimate partner** – This is a love that's magnified between two people. Our intimate partner can make us feel certain, protected and safe, kind of like our parents did for us as children. This is a love that begins the foundation of a life for two people. This could be a love that's shared on a deep and spiritual level. This is a love of *choice* – two people have chosen to be together to share life's experiences. This love can also be replaced or supplemented by a spiritual love – the love of a God or a higher being.

- **Love of children** – This is where most people experience reciprocated unconditional love. (This, of course, can change as children get older.) You love your child and they love you, regardless of what happens. Your children are a part of you; they are your blood. They are reliant on you; you are their support and they need you to survive. It's a connection and a bond like no other. For those who don't have children, this can also be deeply felt with pets.

Each feeling of love is *very* different to the others. If you compare loving a child and loving a spouse, they are very different feelings. Your child is a part of you forever. No matter what happens, your child will always be your child. By contrast, you can have a number of partners throughout your life.

Depending on what stage of life we are in, our priorities will differ regarding which type of love we feel we need to draw from the most.

If you imagine each type of love is represented by a bucket, the first bucket is one that only you can fill, while the other three buckets are reliant on love from other people. At any time, any one of these external buckets can be metaphorically kicked over by someone else, leaving that category of love depleted. This is why it's so important to have a strong foundation of self-love, or a full first bucket.

Do we need all four buckets full to feel totally loved?

Ali is a single mum. She was happy in her life and had three of her love buckets full – she was very confident, she had the love of her child and she had the love of her family and others. She also had a lot of outside interests, including sport and other activities, which kept her very busy.

Even though she was happy, she felt the love of an intimate partner was missing. She signed up to an online dating site and, after a little while, she met Brad. In a short time, she escalated from being happy in life to being ecstatic. It wasn't until she found the love of an intimate partner that she felt complete.

When she was single, she didn't *need* the love of an intimate partner, however, once she felt his love, she realised what she was missing. She was able to take her existing love and magnify it to another level.

As you can see, we don't need love in all of the four buckets to feel happy, but some of us may want all four buckets full to feel truly fulfilled.

Chapter 10: Self-love, self-esteem and self-confidence

This can change at different stages of our lives. At some point, we can feel content with having some of our buckets full, then, all of a sudden, we can develop an urge or desire to focus on the buckets that don't feel complete. Something triggers us to identify a void in our life that we want filled. It could be that we decide that we want a partner, or we want a child, or we could want a dog or a cat. At the end of the day, we all have needs and urges, and we look to fill those needs at the appropriate time. As humans, we try to fill our love buckets the very best way we can, to feel love and connection at the highest level.

~ What masculine men say ~

Gordon was married for over ten years. He had a series of girlfriends after his marriage breakup and always jumped from one relationship to the next, never really thinking about who or what he really wanted. He just knew that he didn't want to be alone. As a result, every time he became single, he got with the very next girl he could. He was always in the wrong relationship.

Thankfully, he realised this and he made some powerful shifts. He acknowledged that it's okay to be alone and that he must strive to love his own company first.

Love buckets and feminine energy

When you are in feminine energy mode, love and connection are your highest needs. This can make a lot of feminine women become overly reliant on filling their need for love from external sources. They rely on their partner, children, friends, phone calls, text messages or social media to make them feel loved. Before long, it can become a massive addiction, where they go wherever they can to get their next 'hit'.

It's very dangerous to rely on outside sources for your happiness. As I mentioned earlier, you have no control over love from those sources, and what's given one day could be taken away the next.

Instead of relying on external sources to fill those needs, you really need to dig deeper into yourself and form a connection with yourself. Get connected with what you want; get connected with your dreams, your hopes, your life and the way you want it. This is *your* life.

Yes, sometimes you can feel unloved and sad. However, the reason this happens is because you've prioritised love from external sources above your love for yourself.

You need to stabilise the love you have for yourself first. If only one of your four buckets was depleted of love, for example, a relationship ended and your love from an intimate partner was taken away, you would still be able to function. It's when that bucket has been your primary focus that your life could start to feel empty.

To accommodate the change and be happy, focus on *you* and filling your self-love bucket first.

As children, we are taught to share and we are taught not to be selfish. We are taught to think of others. However, we also need to remember to love ourselves and to look after ourselves. We need to balance the two.

Putting yourself first doesn't mean you take something from someone else; it's about taking care of yourself and your family. It's only once you take care of yourself that you will have the strength and love to take care of others.

What if your love bucket is controlled by your partner?

Are you relying solely on the love of your intimate partner to feel loved?

This is unsustainable. What if that person told you they were going to end the relationship? They would metaphorically kick over the bucket that held their love, taking their love away from you. What would you have left?

As feminine women, when we believe we have found Mr Right, we can expect him to become our main source of love. This leaves us constantly looking for signals that he loves us. If we focus those expectations towards him, it can literally consume us.

But relying on our man as the main source of our love is dangerous. It's dangerous for our emotional wellbeing and our happiness. We give someone else power over us. It's also not fair on him. Why should he have the sole responsibility of making us feel loved? It's not his job.

We need to focus on us and our own emotional wellbeing. We can't be at peace and we can't be happy when our minds are focused solely on him.

Feminine energy thrives on love and connection. We crave them and, just for the record, we would like to have our man's focus a great deal of the time, or at least know he's thinking about us.

We crave his attention more if we're unhappy within ourselves. If we're not feeling secure and centred, we may constantly think about him. Sometimes we might seem obsessed. We want to see him, we want to speak to him, we want to hear from him. We want to know that he's alright. We want to imagine that he's thinking about us just as much as we are thinking about him.

If we transfer all of our attention to wanting love from our man, our children, our family or our friends instead of ourselves, we will never feel fulfilled at the deepest level. We will feel insecure, uncertain or needy. We will crumble at the thought of them not loving us the way we want to be loved.

Yes, love from an intimate partner can feel awesome because feminine energy wants to fill her love bucket. When she's experiencing true love and she's on a high with her partner, she wants to feel more of it. His love is like a drug – she craves the feelings that make her feel good and she doesn't want them to end. It consumes her so much that if she feels that her man doesn't feel the same way, her heart aches. It can even affect her stability.

Banish The Bitch And Bring Out The Babe

On the other side of the equation is the man. He's totally busy in his world, oblivious to our feelings. He's hard at work and focused on what he's doing. He's in the zone and he doesn't allow himself to be distracted. For the majority of the time, he honestly doesn't think to call us. Despite how we may feel, he's not ignoring us; he's just busy.

He loves connecting with us too, but he doesn't feel the need to all the time. Unlike a feminine woman, who wants to fill up on love, a masculine man wants to release. Once he has released his emotions and he feels loved-up and content, he can go away and finish whatever he needs to finish. When he feels loved-up, he's ready to get onto the next project.

Ultimately, it's not about you. Masculine energy just has different needs to feminine energy.

Some days you just want to be loved. Some days you will long for his attention – if things go wrong, when you feel sad, when you don't feel loved or when you just want a hug. That's okay… Just know that you can't always rely singularly on his love.

This is why it's important to do everything we can to ensure he is not solely responsible for making us feel loved. By filling our self-love bucket first, that love can then overflow to the other buckets.

Love buckets and break ups

If your partner breaks up with you, use your love buckets to help you get through the hurt. The first thing we need to do is get your mind off him. Take your focus off the intimate partner love bucket and focus your energy on your self-love bucket. This will help if you really visualise yourself physically taking your attention away from his bucket.

Don't let his bucket control your emotions, because if you focus your attention there, you will hurt a whole lot more.

Think about what you can do for yourself now. Devise a way where you can get your centre back. You may decide to begin an exercise regime, go on a clean eating plan or go for massages. Decide to do something for you.

Next thing you need to do, is spend some time in the other love buckets. Ring or go and see some of your friends, hug your children or hug your pets.

Use the love of yourself and the love of others to get you through.

If you are arguing and you are not sure if your relationship is over with your man, whatever you do, don't flick the switch and go into your masculine energy. If you do, you could very well say and do things that you will regret later. Be calm.

It's okay to love yourself

We've been taught that it's wrong to love ourselves. People usually think of loving yourself as a sign of conceit or arrogance.

However, self-love is essential for true happiness. In order to be happy in ourselves, we can't rely on outside people for love. We must look for ways to have our own incredible life experiences and build a strong connection to who we are. This then gives us the power to make the right decisions for ourselves because, if we truly love ourselves, why would we do anything that isn't in our best interests? You wouldn't knowingly put your child into a damaging situation or encourage them to spend time with people who are a bad influence, so why would you do that to yourself?

You also can't totally love another until you have made peace with yourself.

There's a difference between self-love and cocky arrogance. Cocky arrogance is an external demonstration designed to get attention. Self-love is internal. Self-love is a deep, unshakable respect for yourself and confidence in yourself.

When you love yourself, you're comfortable with yourself. You live by your values and you know that you're doing the best you can with what you have. You have high standards for yourself and others in your life, and you don't lower them.

Love is the ultimate gift that you can give yourself.

Banish The Bitch And Bring Out The Babe

Make a commitment to YOU

Imagine if you had to get married to yourself before you could marry anyone else. That committing to a loving relationship with yourself is a prerequisite to having a committed relationship with anyone else.

You can make this commitment in your own private ceremony. You can wear a ring that symbolises your love for yourself. It doesn't have to be anything flashy – it could even be a ring you already own.

Go to the beach or park or somewhere private you love. Take deep breaths until you feel at one with your surroundings. Take deep breaths and feel gratitude and love for yourself.

Take the ring and simply say to yourself:

'With this ring, I solemnly declare to love myself in sickness and in health, for richer or poorer, as long as I shall live.'

Then say, 'I do'!

A healthy, loving relationship with ourselves is one where we just make a deal that we will become the best version of ourselves that we can be.

Can I really be happy by myself?

You will have down days. Everyone does. Expect them! You can prepare for them by always being open to receive. Always be open to the universe bringing something to you – compliments, love, friendships, gifts... You never know what might be around the corner.

More importantly, though, you *can* make yourself happy. You can take care of yourself and your emotional wellbeing. Rather than relying on the outside world to make you happy – waiting for someone to call

Chapter 10: Self-love, self-esteem and self-confidence

you, text you, spend time with you or make you feel loved – you can fill your own love bucket.

Here are just some ideas to make yourself feel loved and happy:

- Let someone know how much you love them.
- Have a long, hot soak in the bath.
- Laugh.
- Drive where there's beautiful scenery.
- Listen to your favourite music.
- Sleep in.
- Remember that there is nobody like you in the world – no one!
- Talk to a friend for hours.
- Make new friends or spend time with old ones.
- Have someone play with your hair.
- Get a long head massage.
- Have your favourite chocolate.
- Give a gift that you know someone will love.
- Watch your favourite band.
- Go to a comedy night.
- Lick the cake bowl.
- Smile at a stranger.
- Watch the sunrise or sunset.
- Be grateful for everything you have.
- Remind your friends of how much they mean to you.
- Learn something new (the guitar, singing, another language, cooking, dancing…)
- Walk along the beach.
- Take a book to the park.

- Have a picnic.
- Explore nature.
- Meditate.

What do *you* like to do?

Remember that there will be tough times, and taking care of yourself is a way to prepare your mind, to get stronger. Imagine you are like a squirrel collecting his nuts. You are collecting your nuts, or storing up your energy, so you can then draw on them to get you through the winter. After all, sometimes you need big kahunas to get through tough times. You need to build up the strength and collect the courage to do what needs to be done.

You are mentally preparing for your mind to catch up. You can make your body go through the motions, and before you know it, your mind will accept what's happening.

Are there some hobbies that you could turn into a business? Could you write a book? Is there something that you are great at that you could teach someone else to do? What *could* be your dream? It's never too late to start a new dream. It's never too late to reinvent yourself. Look at Colonel Sanders – he was almost broke and in his sixties when he opened his first KFC franchise. At a time in his life when others were slowing down, he was building an empire. It's never too late.

If a business is not what you have in mind, look for a hobby you would love.

While you're adding these nourishing things to your life, let go of the things that no longer serve you. Declutter and get rid of the useless items that you don't need or want anymore. Put them on eBay or give them away to charity. Give them to someone who needs them and who is going to appreciate them. Cleanse your life and cleanse your soul.

Every day, your main focus should be on how you can be happy. How can you be happy in any given situation? How you can be grateful? How can you be happy with the person you are inside? That's happiness.

Chapter 10: Self-love, self-esteem and self-confidence

Your goal is to be so happy within yourself that you don't need anyone else to feel happy. That's what true self-love is about.

Reclaim your identity

When I separated from Mr Beige, I had a difficult time finding myself. I felt different, I felt lonely and it kind of felt wrong to be alone. I had never been alone before, as I had moved straight from living with my parents to moving in with Mr Beige.

After we separated, I didn't only leave my husband. I left my business. I left my home. I left my city. I left my career. I left my family. I started everything anew.

Yet I struggled for a long time to find my balance and I didn't know why. When I analysed what was happening, I realised that I'd forgotten who I was. I had lost my identity. I was no longer a wife or a business owner. I did not feel successful anymore. Success had previously been a big part of my identity – I relied on it for my certainty, my significance, my growth, my love and connection, and my contribution. Those things felt like they were no longer there.

I realised that I needed to find a new identity. Who was I now? Who had I become?

I couldn't figure it out, and I felt lost.

I had to get my mind right.

Eventually, I asked myself, 'Who am I?' and made myself answer in writing. I began writing: I am a business woman, I am a leader, I am a partner, I am a friend, I am a sister, I am a great person, I am an entrepreneur, I am a skilled producer, I am a visionary, I am a role model, I am an inspiration, I am happy, I am strong, I am centred, I am brave.

When all four of your love buckets are full, it makes it easier to retain your sense of identity. However, when you rely too much on any one type of love (particularly the love of your partner), it can be easy to forget who you are.

One of the biggest mistakes women make is making their life about their man. When we start to date a man and we're in love, we want to be with him all the time. We tend to want to make our lives about him. We can even put our lives on hold, thinking about that fantasy.

In the meantime, we feel paralysed, worried in case we make the wrong move. If we are considering moving, changing the children's school, going travelling or making another big change, we think, 'But what if we get together?'

Before long, we end up 'what iffing' our lives away.

This can be detrimental to our self-esteem, our self-respect, our personal interests, our friendships and more. It could also damage the relationship itself, as we stop being the woman he fell in love with.

Instead, we need to keep moving on with our lives. It doesn't mean that we don't think about our partner. It doesn't mean they're not in our thoughts. We just don't need to obsess. We need to enjoy our time when we're not with him as well as the time we spend with him. Be present when you are without him.

> *You need to focus on you and your life when he is focusing on him and his life.*

While being in a relationship is a part of your identity, it isn't your only role. I can't stress how important it is to have an identity outside your relationship. You aren't just a girlfriend, partner or wife. You have the capacity to be, do and have many other things.

You must make sure that, through life, you don't let go of who you are and what you stand for. For example, I am my own person above and beyond anything else. My partner and my son are in my world and they are a massive part of my world. However, I still make sure I have my own interests and I'm living my own values and desires. I live for my goals, my dreams and my aspirations, and I include my son, partner, family and friends in those. Sure, your life's path can change over time, but you just need to stay true to yourself.

It's time to reclaim your identity. It's time to feel whole. It's time to be you again.

Your identity is who you see yourself as today and who you're going to be in future. It can be whoever you want to be.

> **Who are you?**
>
> Think about who you are and who you want to be. Take a moment to write down anything that comes to you – you might write descriptive words, you might write things you want to achieve or experience, you might write the names of women you want to emulate.
>
> Don't censor yourself. Remember to think big. If you keep going, you will unlock many ideas for yourself. This exercise is where I came up with the solid idea of writing this book.
>
> Once you've made your list, create a daily ritual of programming your mind to remember who you are or who you want to become. Simply create a shortlist of the most powerful items on your list and rewrite them as incantations, each one starting with the words 'I am'. For example:
>
> - I am smart.
> - I am a kick-ass business woman.
> - I am funny.
> - I am amazing.
> - I am fun, sexy and feminine.
> - I am feminine, fit and fantastic.
> - I am successful, happy and energised.
> - I am an awesome mum, wife and business person.
>
> Start every morning with your incantations. Make a lovely poster to put in your bathroom or even just put them on post-it notes on your mirror. Read them every day.

You need to instil and cement your identity until it becomes ingrained at a cellular level. When it truly becomes your identity, your mind, body and soul will believe it.

And once you recognise who you are, you can turn your focus to what you want.

What do you want for your life?

It's easy to get so focused on finding a man that we forget about the other things we want for our lives. If our man is our only purpose or vision, that makes it hard to establish and maintain our own identity.

Yet the question of what you want to build, do or create can feel a little overwhelming. It can also put you into your masculine energy, as you get very focused on your goal and mapping out the steps to achieve it.

Instead, I would like to demonstrate the life wheel exercise, which I learnt about through Anthony Robbins.

The life wheel

On a blank piece of paper, draw a circle and divide it into seven equal parts. Give the sections the following labels:

- Physical health
- Finances
- Career
- Emotions
- Spirituality
- Relationships (partner, family and friends)

Chapter 10: Self-love, self-esteem and self-confidence

> Each segment represents one of these areas, with the point in the centre of the wheel representing a lack of fulfilment, or zero percent fulfilment, and the outer edge representing 100 percent fulfilment in that area. In each segment, draw a line to indicate where you think you rate for each topic.
>
> This will show if your life wheel is unbalanced. If it is, you are probably having a little bit of a bumpy ride. It's time to work on all of those areas of your life. Little by little.

If you struggle with the life wheel exercise, ask yourself the following questions about your life to help you assess each area:

- What do you *want* to do?
- What *could* you do?
- Who can help you and what resources do you have?
- What past experiences have you had that have made you the person you are today?
- What empowering beliefs do you need?
- Who do you want to become?
- Why do you want to become this person?
- What will it give you?
- How will it change your life?
- How will you affect others by being this person?
- How many people could you inspire and help by becoming this new empowered person?

Once you have recorded this, then work out a way you can bridge the gap to get from where you are to feeling 100 percent in this area.

Banish The Bitch And Bring Out The Babe

Looking back on your life

Find a peaceful place and take a deep breath. Close your eyes. Connect with yourself, your thoughts and your wishes.

Think about what you really want for your life.

Close your eyes and imagine being eighty-five years old. If you could rewind your life, what would you love to see? What would you love to have accomplished?

Write down the answers to the following:

- What do you admire about yourself (it doesn't matter if it's just a small a thing)? Do you like your hair, your legs, your eyes, your strength, your caring nature, or something else?
- What are you good at?
- If you can't see anything right now, what *could* you love?
- What do others love about you?
- What could they love about you?

Build your self-esteem and self-confidence

Self-esteem is the final piece of this puzzle. Self-esteem is the level of respect and appreciation you have for yourself. While it is linked to and influenced by your self-love and sense of identity, it's also distinct so deserves its own discussion.

Without a doubt, the older we get, the more self-confidence we have. We've experienced more, learnt about ourselves and the world, and usually have a track record of successes behind us. We've learnt our capabilities. We recognise the consequences of any of our actions. We know what we want. We know our boundaries. We know whom we can trust. We learn to trust our own judgements. We have a solid belief in ourselves.

However, this belief and confidence can be damaged by others if we aren't careful about whose opinions we take on board.

Donna is very attractive, feminine and a lovely person. However, she was constantly belittled by her husband. He would repeatedly tell her that she was fat and ugly and that, if ever they separated, she would never attract another man. He did this so that she would never have the confidence to leave him. It was the only way he thought that he could make her stay.

Low self-esteem originates from not loving yourself. That's it. If you suffer from low self-esteem, you are probably relying on external sources to feel loved, rather than filling up your love buckets yourself.

If you are feeling low, you could have also convinced yourself that no one loves you. Your whole life could be occupied with hoping to get love and connection from others. You'll find yourself hoping that someone phones you, messages you or makes contact with you. If and when they do, you may allow yourself to feel loved. If no one calls you, you may allow yourself to feel unloved.

This is no way to live. You can't live on the edge of your seat waiting for others to make you feel happy and make you feel loved.

You must learn to feel love within yourself. You must be an individual and be your own person.

If anyone says something negative about you

If anyone says something negative about you, it could affect your 'love from others' bucket. It could hurt you, depending on how much love you have in that bucket to start with.

You take on beliefs from a range of sources. Sometimes they come from within, as you think that you are your behaviour and you label yourself as that. If you have done something stupid, you call yourself stupid.

No, you're not. It's just something you did. You are not stupid or a bad person. It's not your identity. Sometimes you simply just need to make better choices.

The same thing can happen when other people criticise you. If someone said when you were younger that you weren't good at spelling or you weren't good at maths, you could have taken their thoughts or judgements on board. It could have been your parents or your teacher who said something. Maybe it wasn't even true but you took it on board anyway. It could have even become part of your identity. Do you have BS references based on something someone else said about you?

Why do we form an opinion of ourselves and give ourselves an identity based on other people's perceptions of us? They were only someone else's thoughts or perceptions of their reality at a particular point in time. Why is someone else's opinion of us more important than our own opinion of ourselves?

Great leaders, those who believe in themselves and those who believe in what they are doing, don't let other people sway them. They might feel the feelings, but they push forward regardless. They know who they are, and they know what they want.

During my relationship with Mr Small, I consistently weighed between 56 and 58kgs, which is great for my height. I always felt awesome at that weight. However, even though I felt great and I felt I looked great, Mr Small constantly told me I should be 52kgs and that I needed all kinds of plastic surgery and Botox. He researched procedures and consistently sent me emails about it. It hurt to think he was judging me constantly, especially when I thought I looked good (and generally we are our own toughest critics).

There is no reason for you to take on what others think of you.

Dr Wayne Dyer had a great approach for dealing with others' negativity and criticism. He said that when his children had trouble with someone calling them a name, he asked them, 'If someone gave you a gift and you didn't accept it, whom would it belong to?' They said, 'It belongs to the person who gave it to you.' In the same way, if someone gives you the gift of calling you a bad name and you don't accept it, it belongs to them.

> *'Opinions are like assholes; everyone has one.'* And just because you have one, it doesn't mean I want to see or hear yours.

It's none of your business what other people think of you. What if someone said you were a truck – and you know you're not a truck – what would you think? You wouldn't take on that identity, so why should you take on any other identity they try to give you?

We are the only ones who know who we are deep down inside. Only we know who we really are in our hearts and only we know what we are truly capable of.

If you are going to take on others' opinions of you, make sure they are people who make you feel good about yourself. If they put you down, call you names, or say you should be thinner... run a mile! You don't need them. Find people who will cherish and respect you.

Ultimately, don't acknowledge the negative things people say about you. If you always analyse what others think of you, you will always feel like you're in conflict. Some people will approve of what you do, others won't. Not everyone will fly Qantas and not everyone will fly Virgin. People will have different opinions for all sorts of reasons.

When decisions are controlled by what you perceive everyone is going to think or say about you, you will *not* be happy. The only thing that matters is what you think of yourself. Focus on making *you* happy.

What do you REALLY think of yourself?

If you were to picture yourself back when you were a happy baby or small child, who were you? Picture your smiling face; picture your cute, little hands and feet. Picture your beautiful, little eyes and smile. You were a perfect, innocent, little child.

Now, remember a little further forward in your life, when you were a teenager growing up, before you got involved in relationships, before children and before work got in the way. What did you love to do? Swimming, bike riding, surfing, walking, dancing, kayaking, going out with friends, going to the movies? What are some things that you wanted to do when you grew up that you haven't done as yet?

Fast forward to today. Do you know that, today, you are as perfect as you always have been? You are perfect just the way you are. You are perfect for what's happened to you, your life experiences, your situation and the choices you've made. You are a perfect example of what has shaped you. You have a history and that's reflected in who you are now. All those pieces are *you* and there is nobody else like you. Nobody.

Something that may benefit you in this section is some closed-eye processes we have in our online course at http://banishthebitch.com/online-course/

If you are struggling to be yourself, think of this story:

A little boy went into a pet shop to buy a little dog with his birthday money. He looked at the dogs in the cages for a while before the salesperson came and offered the boy assistance. The salesperson asked if he had picked out the puppy he wanted.

'Yes, sir,' said the boy, 'That one there. He's adorable, I love him.'

The shop assistant said, 'Oh no, you don't want that one; he's got a bad leg. He can't walk properly and you will have nothing but trouble with him. He's more trouble than he's worth. We will probably put him out of his misery and get him put down.'

Chapter 10: Self-love, self-esteem and self-confidence

The boy looked at the man with tears in his eyes and said, 'In that case, I will definitely have him then.' With that, the boy walked over to the counter to pay. The boy had a limp and had callipers on his leg.

You never know what someone is going to like about you and why. Don't make judgements about yourself, speculating what other people like or don't like.

Don't change so people will like you – be yourself and the right people will love the real you.

> ### ♀♂ Anchor to your feminine energy – Connect to your feminine energy.
>
> Clench your left fist. Feel every word whilst you read the section below.
>
> If you have one of our *Banish The Bitch* bracelets, wear it on your left wrist. Feel the bracelet acting as an anchor and allow it to store and remind you of the feelings below.
>
> If you need to feel these feelings throughout the day, simply clench your left fist or wear your bracelet on your left wrist to re-establish your anchor.
>
> Go into your heart.
>
> The secret to self-love is forgiveness. It is about forgiving yourself and it is about forgiving others. It is about living in peace. If you have made some decisions that you have not come to terms with, you need to forgive yourself for everything and move on in life. There is no point beating yourself up every day for things you can't change. Those decisions taught you valuable lessons and made you the person you are today.
>
> Please take out a piece of paper and write down all the things you could forgive yourself for.

> Make a list of everyone else that you could also forgive in the process and what you are forgiving them for. This exercise will amaze you! Keep writing and writing. You don't need to tell them – just write it for yourself.
>
> I forgive…
>
> I forgive…
>
> I forgive…
>
> This process really helps you articulate how you feel. After you have said everything you want to say, I would suggest that you burn your note and say goodbye to the feelings you felt.

How to get back into your power

When my first relationship ended, I put on a lot of weight, I cut my hair short and I wore unflattering glasses. I simply stopped trying to look nice.

I subconsciously wanted to prevent any future relationships from happening, to protect myself from experiencing the same hurt again; I hid behind a wall of kilograms and a huge number of barriers.

What I didn't realise was that I had really compromised myself. I needed to start loving myself again.

These patterns can show up in every area of our lives. You can unknowingly sabotage your own success and your own happiness – you might stop pursuing creative passions that are important to you, you might stop spending time with your friends and family, you might stop learning and growing or, like I did, you might stop loving your body. What we forget is that these areas are all a part of *us*, and we need to make them a priority for ourselves regardless of what's happening in our romantic relationships.

This is the cornerstone of self-esteem.

> ♂ **Anchor to your masculine energy – Connect to your masculine energy.**
>
> Clench your right fist. Feel every word whilst you read the section below.
>
> If you have one of our *Banish The Bitch* bracelets, wear it on your right wrist. Feel the bracelet acting as an anchor and allow it to store and remind you of the feelings below.
>
> If you need to feel these feelings throughout the day, simply clench your right fist or wear your bracelet on your right wrist to re-establish your anchor.
>
> Develop some power words that you can focus on. These words need to be written down and must be clearly visible for you to see every day. Put them on your bathroom mirror where you will be constantly reminded of them.
>
> These are words that will help you get into a confident state of mind. Some examples are love, strength, power, self-love, centred, self-control and responsibility.
>
> Think of some words that excite you or make you feel good. Think of one word at a time that makes you feel good or makes you feel strong.
>
> When you look at these words, I want you to feel the feelings. I want you to associate with these feelings and know that you can access them at any time.

Be grateful for what you have

I met a lovely single mum recently at the beach one day. On talking to her, I found out that she had two children and one of her children, her ten-year-old daughter, had a life-threatening illness. They'd experienced an incredibly tough time over the last six years, and all she wanted was to make her daughter better. My heart went out to her.

When you feel a bit down and sad with the world, remember there are always people much worse off than you. I'm so incredibly grateful for everything in my life and sometimes it takes another perspective to make you even more grateful.

Make a decision to be happy with yourself right now. Be happy for all you have accomplished and all you have done. Give yourself a pat on the back for where you are now.

Heal yourself with gratitude

Write out what you're grateful for. Simply write down: 'I'm grateful for...' and finish the sentence with whatever you feel grateful for.

- I am grateful for my son, my health, my body, my appearance and my eyesight.
- I am grateful that I can walk, run and hear.
- I am grateful for my family.
- I am grateful for my friends.
- I am grateful for the opportunities I have in my life.
- I am grateful for the mistakes I have made and the lessons I have learnt from them.

We need to appreciate and feel grateful for the love we do have in our lives, rather than focusing on what we feel is missing from our lives.

Becoming an even better YOU

Sadly, women in this day and age are rarely happy with themselves. We are much more critical than men about our abilities, the way we act and the way we look, and it can sometimes weigh heavily on our self-esteem.

Chapter 10: Self-love, self-esteem and self-confidence

If you *are* happy with yourself, embrace this – it will leave you feeling empowered and confident.

If you are not the way you would like to be, what can you do to change so you feel happier? Remember, this should be about what *you* want, not what you think a man might want.

Then consider: Why haven't you done this already? Do you associate any pain with changing? Is there anything you will gain from staying the way you are? What needs are you filling with your current behaviour?

I am not a dietician and you need to seek your own advice, but I would like to share my weight loss experience, since losing weight made such a big difference for me.

When it comes to food, many of us don't eat because we're hungry. Instead, we use food to fill other needs.

If you regularly meet friends for lunch, dinner, and coffee and cake, eating could be a hugely pleasurable social exercise. This can make giving up these experiences even harder, as it's not only the food – it is about the whole experience. When you meet with your friends, you experience a social connection. You talk to them, you learn about each other, you feel special, you have a laugh and you experience love and connection. You could very well be addicted to the feelings these catch-ups give you.

Or perhaps you're eating to smother uncomfortable or difficult emotions. When I put on weight, food became an anchor for my emotions. It got to the stage where, when I felt lonely, bored, unhappy or any other negative emotion, I would eat to make myself feel better. At the same time, I thought that my body should be strong enough to deal with coffee, junk food, alcohol or anything else I might put in it. In reality, it wasn't.

How do you feel when you eat? If you are comfort eating, what are you upset about? Are you lonely? Are you bored? Are you sad? What is it really? I was in a state of uncertainty. When I was worried about something, I ate because I knew it was certain to make me feel good, even if that was only in the short-term.

What changed? Sometimes you can have a situation where the straw breaks the camel's back. It's when you get past a certain point and you feel like you must change. For me, this happened when I was going out for dinner with some girlfriends. I got into my friends' car and thought I heard my pants split, but I felt around and couldn't feel anything. It was only once I got to the restaurant that I realised it was true – I had split my pants up the back! Luckily, one of my girlfriends had a hotel sewing kit in her bag, and I went into the bathroom at the restaurant and proceeded to sew my pants up. I never want to go through that ever again.

I then began the process of making healthier food choices over time. I started by not drinking coffee, then I cut out desserts, then I made sure I ate plenty of salads and vegetables, then I only bought dark chocolate with stevia instead of sugar.

Once I did those things, I started feeling great about myself and could then muster even more strength and determination. I began to tell myself, 'If I can't control what I put in my own mouth, how can I have any influence over anything else?'

The changes continued – I exercised. I ate more protein. I ate healthy. On a Sunday, I used to have a bit of a splurge – a relaxing day off the eating plan. I began to love my body again. By taking care of myself, the weight just dropped off. I felt great again. I showed myself I had the discipline and I also showed myself how good I could look.

If there's something you would like to change or improve to become your best self, the best place to start is getting clear on *why* you want to change. When I was focused on getting into shape, some of my motivators were:

- I must be a great role model for my son in healthy eating.
- I will never love myself if I don't love my body.
- If I can't control myself with discipline and leadership, I won't be able to control anything else.
- I will never be a great role model or inspiration to anyone if I don't.

Chapter 10: Self-love, self-esteem and self-confidence

- When I get momentum with my body, I get momentum in my life.
- If I feel overweight, I don't feel like a feminine woman – I feel like a slob.
- I can be more determined and disciplined than those around me because I'm strong.
- I care about the little things I do – eating and drinking loads of water.

> **What's your 'why'?**
>
> How do you want to look and how do you want to feel better?
>
> Get a piece of paper and list all the reasons you can think of.
>
> How will changing improve your self-esteem, self-confidence and self-love? How will it improve your relationship with your partner and children (if you have any)? How could it change other areas of your life?

If the change you want to make is losing some weight, some general food tips include: (See your doctor or health professional first)

- Start with the small things. Have the determination and the discipline to do what you know you need to do.
- Keep a food journal for a week. I use an app called myfitnesspal – I love it. If you look back after a week and see that you have eaten a lot of chocolate, pizza, McDonald's, ice cream, cake and coffee, that's a clear indication of where any excess weight has come from. Once you see these crappy food options, replace them with healthier alternatives.
- Make some rules around eating. For example, I made a rule that I didn't eat after 7:30pm, so I brushed my teeth

Banish The Bitch And Bring Out The Babe

at 7:30pm. I didn't drink soft drinks, eat chocolate or drink alcohol. I also had rules that I had to drink plenty of water and herbal teas, and eat plenty of salads and vegetables. I didn't have any junk food. I did not eat big meals at night. My body felt better not going to bed on a heavy stomach.

- Aim to do some exercise first thing in the morning. This will kick start your metabolism for the day, it will affirm how much you care about your health, it will clear your mind, and it will build confidence as you will have already achieved something for the day.

- If you feel that you have sugar cravings, it can be helped by having coconut oil – just a tablespoon a day. Also look for healthier options that you can have instead of sugar, such as stevia.

- If food helps you meet social needs, you don't need to give up the social experience – you can just make some slight changes. Research restaurants that serve healthier alternatives. You could also meet for a different activity, such as going for a walk or going to a gym instead of meeting at a restaurant. Try to inspire your friends to help you, and you'll be helping them in turn.

Dream board

Get really, really excited about your future. We've all heard the saying from the Bible: 'Without a vision, people perish'. We are now going to create a vision for your life. Go to your local newsagency or stationary supplier and buy a big sheet of cardboard. Next, we are going to design a poster with pictures of all the things that you love. Things that you want to attract into your life. Whether that's a house you would love, a car you would love, a body you would love. It can be anything in the world. It doesn't only have to be material things; it can also be any feelings that you want to feel. You are going to let the universe know what you want. You can print your pictures off the Internet.

Chapter 10: Self-love, self-esteem and self-confidence

Here's the deal, though, on your poster, you are not going to play small. You are going to dream big. Because if you are going to dream and have aspirations, you may as well dream HUGE!

What does your new amazing life look like? What does it sound like? Whom will you be with? If you're not sure whom you will be with, whom could you be with? What will you do for fun? Where will you go on holidays? Where would you really love to live? What will the décor be like, what style will your furniture be? What sort of clothes do you want? Whom do you want to be with?

Dream. Dream. Dream. Next, visit some real estate websites and have a look where you would love to live. Upon looking, your initial reaction could be that you can't afford what you love, but that doesn't matter – get some brochures to include on your vision board anyway.

Go to open houses, get a feel for where you could be living if you put your mind to it. Picture your soul mate with you. What does he look like? Do you have children together? Does the house have a pool? What can you see? What can you feel?

And... keep in mind... You don't need to know how you will find the money. That's up to the universe.

In the meantime, if you need to create a feeling of security, if you can, start to save money every week, even if it's only $10 or $20 a week. Put that money in a bank account that you never touch. Aim to save for something special. Have a goal that you can work towards.

Now, if you read this and you think that you don't know what you want – that's okay... Sometimes it's hard to see what you DO want. Sometimes your mind needs to be in the right place. Over the next few days, I want you to think about what you don't want in your life. I want you to get really associated with what you DON'T want.

For example – If you don't want to work at a particular place, if you don't want to work nights or if you don't want to live in a caravan/trailer park. Get clear on the things that you don't want. Sometimes you need to think about what you don't want in order to know what you do want.

249

Summary

If only I knew then what I know now...

- Guard your identity; remember who you are. Never forget it. You have to know who you really are in your core. Your identity must be unshakable.

- You have to love yourself. It's not negotiable. Loving yourself is not being arrogant, or thinking that you are better than anyone else; it means that you are kind to yourself and that you make decisions that are good for you. It's all about taking care of yourself.

- Know that your partner can be your rock and they can be your strength when things are great. They can also be your kryptonite or your weakness when things are tough between you. When you have rough times in your relationship, it's not wise to only rely on your partner for love. You need to create other permanent foundations of love to hold you up.

- Your self-confidence is everything. What you think about yourself matters the most. Don't worry about what others say – their opinions don't mean a thing. Don't take other people's opinions on board unless they serve you.

- Do everything that you can to feel great about the person you are. If there is something you don't like about yourself and it's making you miserable, if you can, change it.

- Always remember that you are a good person, no matter what happens. Sometimes you may make the wrong decisions. It doesn't mean that you are dumb, it just means that you made a decision that wasn't your best option at the time. Always try to make better choices and stop beating yourself up. Learn from them.

Exercises

1. What can you do to make you happy? You need to do loving, nurturing things for yourself. You must take care of yourself emotionally, physically and spiritually.

2. One way you can get into a great state of mind is to say incantations. Get yourself into a happy state by going for a brisk walk or a jump on a trampoline and say positive incantations like: 'I am smart,' 'I am funny,' 'I am amazing,' 'I love myself,' 'I have the man of my dreams,' 'I am fulfilled,' 'I am awesome,' and 'I am feminine, fun, fit and fantastic.'

3. Start exercising.

4. Take a few minutes a day to remind yourself of everything that you are grateful for.

5. Support is important. Develop a support group of people you can call for a chat. Go out and meet people. Go to meet-up groups. For now, compile a list of people that you will keep in contact with – aim for twenty people to get started and work your way up to fifty people. It can either be your fifty closest friends or fifty people that you would like to have as close friends. These people will help you feel better and help you overcome any feelings of loneliness.

6. From today, make a commitment for one month to actively look for things you love to do. Say yes to life. Look to learn new things. You'll experience things you may not have experienced and you'll meet people you wouldn't have met.

7. Watch inspirational/motivational videos, even if it's only for five minutes.

8. Think back to all you have done in the last ten years. Write a quick list of things you have achieved. Write down five things that you accomplished that you never thought you would, no matter how insignificant they may seem.

Conclusion: It's your time

Take a chance. Do what you love to do – you never know whom you are going to inspire.

It had been some time since Jack had seen Mr Besler. College, girls, his career and life itself got in the way. Jack had moved clear across the country in pursuit of his dreams. In the rush of his busy life, Jack had little time to think about the past and often no time to spend with his wife and son. He was working on his future, and nothing could stop him.

Over the phone, his mother told him, 'Mr Besler died last night. The funeral is on Wednesday.'

Memories flashed through Jack's mind like an old newsreel as he remembered his childhood days.

'Jack, did you hear me?'

'Oh, sorry, mum. Yes, I heard you. It's been so long since I thought of him. I'm sorry, but I honestly thought he died years ago,' Jack said.

'Well, he didn't forget you. Every time I saw him, he'd ask how you were doing. He'd reminisce about the many days you spent over "his side of the fence", as he put it,' mum told him.

'I loved that old house he lived in,' Jack said.

'You know, Jack, after your father died, Mr Besler stepped in to make sure you had a man's influence in your life,' she said.

'He's the one who taught me carpentry,' he said. 'I wouldn't be in this business if it weren't for him. He spent a lot of time teaching me things he thought were important... I'll be there for the funeral.'

As busy as he was, he kept his word. Jack caught the next flight to his hometown. Mr Besler's funeral was small and uneventful. He had no children of his own, and most of his relatives had passed away.

The night before he returned home, Jack and his mum stopped by to see the old house next door one more time.

Standing in the doorway, Jack paused for a moment. It was like crossing over into another dimension, a leap through space and time.

The house was exactly as he remembered. Every step held memories. Every picture, every piece of furniture... Jack stopped suddenly.

'What's wrong, Jack?' his mum asked.

'The box is gone,' he said.

'What box?'

'There was a small, gold box that he kept locked on top of his desk. I must have asked him a thousand times what was inside. All he'd ever tell me was, "The thing I value most,"' Jack said.

It was gone. Everything about the house was exactly how Jack remembered it, except for the box. He figured someone from the Besler family had taken it.

'Now I'll never know what was so valuable to him,' Jack said. 'I better get some sleep. I have an early flight home, mum.'

Two weeks later, Jack received a package. The small box was old and looked like it had been mailed a hundred years ago. The handwriting was difficult to read, but the return address caught his attention – 'Mr Harold Besler' it read.

Jack ripped open the package. Inside were the gold box and an envelope. Jack's hands shook as he read the note inside.

'Upon my death, please forward this box and its contents to Jack Bennett. It's the thing I valued most in my life.'

A small key was taped to the letter. His heart racing, tears filling his eyes, Jack carefully unlocked the box. Inside he found a beautiful, gold pocket watch. Running his fingers slowly over the finely-etched casing, he unlatched the cover.

Inside he found these words engraved: 'Jack, thanks for your time! Harold Besler.'

'The thing he valued most was my time,' Jack realised.

After a few moments, Jack called his office and cleared his appointments for the next two days. When his assistant asked why, he said, 'I need some time to spend with my son.'

Story by Bob Perks

With this story, we've come to the end of our journey together. On this journey, we've covered a vast terrain. You've learnt about yourself – your feminine energy, your masculine energy and how to integrate the two to create a life and relationship you love. You've learnt about finding Mr Right – how masculine and feminine energy interact in a relationship, how to become the woman who will attract your knight in shining armour, and how to be irresistible when you enter the dating game. And you've learnt about maintaining or rediscovering your spark once you're in a relationship.

Now that we're here, it's time to get excited about the rest of your life! It's time to look towards your compelling future – one filled with excitement, love and compassion.

There is no reason why you can't have it all. Just because something happened when you were younger, or something happened to someone in your family, it doesn't have to dictate your future. What happened in the past is in the past. Now it is your turn to look towards the horizon.

Change can happen instantly on the path of self-discovery.

When my son was about three years old, I was diagnosed with a genetic blood disease. My GP didn't understand the results and panicked, leaving me certain that I was going to die. I was so scared. I remember looking at my son and thinking, 'Shit! What am I going to do? I can't die. I have to see my little boy grow up and become a man. I just have to.'

Thank goodness it wasn't terminal (the specialist put my mind at ease and explained what I had), and it's all okay. However, I have not been the same person since. I don't sweat the small stuff anymore. I don't worry as much as I used to. I don't worry about making hard decisions if it's the right thing to do. I live how I want to live.

Wake-up calls can change your life. However, that doesn't mean you have to wait for a wake-up call to make a change.

Start to plan a way to work towards where you want to be. Make the most of every single day. Don't wait for anyone or anything. This is *your* life – *you* get to choose how you live.

Take the time to connect – to your feminine energy, to your masculine energy, to the people you love and to life itself. Be focused and directed when you need to be, but also take the time to unwind, feel and *be*.

And, while you're at it, why not register for speed dating or register on an online dating site? Or, if you're in a relationship, organise a romantic getaway with your partner?

Just like the weather, in life, there are seasons. There's winter, spring, summer and autumn. Your life will not always be the way it is now. Sometimes life is incredibly awesome. Sometimes life can feel tough, as it doesn't always go the way we plan. And sometimes life can downright suck.

Sometimes, when times get tough, it's hard to see a future ahead. It's hard to picture how you are going to move forward. Things can seem impossible. Know in your heart that it will work out eventually. This is where faith plays a huge part – eventually everything works itself out, one way or another.

The key is to remember that your time is precious. We have limited time on this earth, so make the most of it! Banish the bitch, bring out the babe, attract the man of your dreams and take this opportunity to live the life you were meant to live.

A message for you...

You have just read what I would have said to my sister.

Linda, unfortunately, passed away a long time ago.

Sadly, Linda never got to experience a sunset, never got to experience love, and she never even got to experience laughter. She never experienced much at all.

Sometimes we forget how incredibly lucky we are to experience life – the ups and downs and all it entails.

Sometimes we complain and we moan.

You know what? We can justify in a multitude of ways why we aren't living the life we should.

The truth is... It's up to us.

You have the opportunity to live your wildest dreams. Figure out what those dreams are, make the commitment to them and get started.

What are you waiting for?

Go and live the life you deserve.

About the author

Lisa understands just how difficult it can be to be a confident woman in this world. After years of hearing that women had given up on trying to find their ideal partners out of frustration, and that men thought women had become too masculine and intimidating, she began to seek out the truth.

What she discovered next truly shocked her: there wasn't any quality information available for women to embrace. She was inspired to write *Banish the Bitch* when she couldn't find a book to teach her what she wanted to learn about masculine and feminine energy and their role in relationships. She immersed herself in the study of masculine and feminine energy in a quest to find balance in life and love. Using her own life as an example, she did away with what was not working to make way for what would.

Lisa is a speaker, trainer, coach and serial entrepreneur who has owned numerous businesses since 1995, experiencing two marriages and starting a family along the way. Her busy life allows her to truly understand the pressures that today's world places on women and their relationships, both at home and in their day-to-day lives.

Lisa has had the pleasure of coaching many women all over the world in masculine and feminine energy, business and life. In the world of self-development, Lisa specialises in integrating masculine and feminine energy to create the perfect foundation for loving, fulfilling relationships.

Banish The Bitch And Bring Out The Babe

Lisa studied psychology at university for two years before becoming an accredited life coach and a qualified NLP master practitioner. She has also studied intensely with Tony Robbins, completing his Mastery University several times as well as becoming a member of his exclusive 'Platinum Partners' group.

She is an established writer, her books include *Secret Agents – How the top real estate agents list more, sell more and dominate the market* – she was featured in the book *Real Estate Millionaire* and she also has her own published columns in a number of magazines.

Lisa lives on the Gold Coast in beautiful Queensland, Australia.

Please message Lisa's team at support@lisab.com.au with your stories about masculine and feminine energy. She would love to hear from you.

Keep In Touch

LinkedIn –
www.linkedin.com/in/lisab007

Facebook –
www.facebook.com/bringoutthebabe

Twitter –
www.twitter.com/bringoutthebabe

Instagram –
www.instagram.com/lisabaustralia

Pinterest –
www.pinterest.com/lisab0007

YouTube –
www.youtube.com/c/Banishthebitchlisab

www.banishthebitch.com/podcast

www.BanishTheBitch.com

lisa@lisab.com.au

www.ingramcontent.com/pod-product-compliance
Lightning Source LLC
Chambersburg PA
CBHW071226080526
44587CB00013BA/1511